NECROPOLIS OF THEBES
1:19.000

0 100 200 300 400 500 600 700 800
Yards.

S

Dēr el-baḥri

North.ⁿ Asasif

Later Tombs

Pyramid

Dēr el-baḥri

Route to the Kings

El-Wādiyēn

Ḳaṣr el-bakhīt

Tomb of Nebamon

T. of Thutmosis III.

T. of Ramses III.

Pal. of Ḥatshepsowet

Drah Abul Negga

Tomb of Siptaḥ

T. of Amenophis I.

PASSAGE
TO
ETERNITY

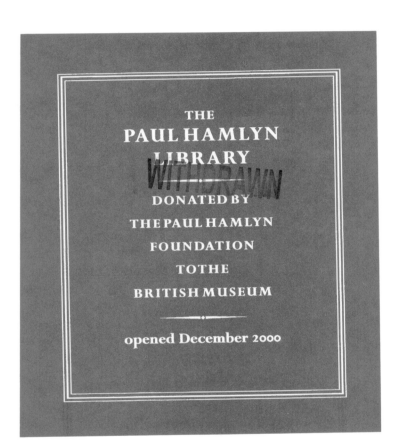

R. WULLEMAN
M. KUNNEN
A. MEKHITARIAN

PASSAGE TO ETERNITY

NYCOMED

TECHNICAL SPECIFICATIONS

ISBN   90-6958-008-X

Texts   *A. Mekhitarian*
Legends   *A. Mekhitarian, R. Wulleman*
Photography   *M. Kunnen, A. Mekhitarian, R. Wulleman*
Layout & typography   *Marc Hutsebaut*
Additional layout   *Geertrui Peeters*
Coordination   *Helmut Weiss*
Translated from French by   *Marc Hutsebaut*
Colour separations   *NV Deckmyn*, Roeselare (Belgium)
Printed by   *NV Vansevenant*, Poperinge (Belgium)

First edition   © *Mappamundi Knokke*, Belgium. October 1989.

MAPPAMUNDI

A French edition of this book has been published simultaneously by *Mappamundi, Knokke* (Belgium), in cooperation with *Les Editions Ozalid*, Paris (France).

TABLE OF CONTENTS

INTRODUCTION

t the beginning of this introductory chapter and to avoid any equivocality, it seemed justified to recall to the reader the way in which this book saw the light. To clarify this we will resort to a comparison. Imagine an abstract painter who, at a given point in time, creates his work drawing from a certain source of inspiration and who only bestows a name on his creations when he intends to exhibit them at an art gallery. Something similar occurred with this book. During a short stay at Luxor, two friends, enamoured of Egypt and photography, enjoy the privilege of taking snapshots in some twenty tombs of the Theban Necropolis. Enchanted with the results, they wish to share their joy with other people and they conceive the creation of a wonderful picture-book. An equally enthusiastic publisher is found willing to take on the publication and orders the preparation of a presentation layout. Of course, by now, the book calls for a title. Since the majority of the scenes to be reproduced describe aspects of the underworld as conceived by the ancient Egyptians, the title *Passage to Eternity* springs up almost naturally. Was this not the very dream the Pharaohs and their people alike cherished during their life-time on earth? With a title likely to cause unintended confusion, though, a few lines which will hopefully clear up misunderstandings, seemed in order. Ergo : this is **not** a scientific publication which systematically explores Egyptian philosophy with respect to life in the hereafter, but a sample collection - quite incomplete - of infernal representations. Although not entirely arbitrary, their choice has depended, more often than not, on considerations of technical quality rather than of religious importance. The insertion of a number of scenes from day-to-day life is easily defensible by the remark that, in some way or other, the Egyptians wished to see their earthly lives perpetuated in the great beyond : living proof of their optimism and joy of living. The four short text chapters, apart from improving the cohesion of the legends to the illustrations, pay a "flying visit" to each of the four selected areas of the Necropolis, sketching, roughly, what is contained within each typical group of tombs. We

hope that our iconographical survey, however concise, combined with some aesthetical observations, will allow the reader to enrich his appreciation of Egyptian drawings, bas-reliefs and paintings during the four centuries of Theban splendour (1500-1100 B.C.). The explanatory comments throughout the volume will further equip the attentive reader with keys to the complex paintings which adorn the royal and private tombs, allowing him to penetrate, slowly but steadily, into the Egyptian way of thinking. This, in (less than) a nutshell, makes up the contents of the conclusion at the end of this book.

Some readers will probably expect that, henceforth, a synthesis of Pharaonic religion will be presented, a synthesis to facilitate the accessibility of the ensuing images. That, however, is far too ambitious a task which only the layman would deem feasible. Anyone who is well or even vaguely acquainted with Egyptology, who has seen the kilometres of inscriptions, bas-reliefs and paintings covering the walls of temples and tombs, who has visited the museums which preserve hundreds of thousands of objects, all worthy of study, knows that every single research programme requires years and years of intense labour, that no archaeologist can pride himself in knowing everything, that, forcibly, specialization in one of the many fields of research which lay open for us, is inevitable. Thus, an authority on the *Book of the Dead*, for instance, will admit unashamedly that the infernal books reproduced on the walls of the royal tombs, appear as enigmatic to him as they might do to anyone unable to read hieroglyphics. Furthermore, venturing to paint an overall picture which the connoisseurs will certainly brush aside as a caricature, is a hazardous operation. Nevertheless, here are some general notions, elements of which will be repeated as and when the occasion arises.

Man has always been intrigued by the genesis of the universe. In Egypt, three theological schools, based in Memphis, Hermopolis and Heliopolis, drew up cosmogonies, of which the one advocating the worship of the sun emerged as the most popular. The heliopolitan system taught that at the origin of things reigned chaos, a kind of primeval ocean named Nun, which sheltered a being called Tum or Atum - meaning at the same time *everything* and *nothing* - who, emerging from the water, became light: he is the sun-god Re. Atum is, in other words, a synonym of Re, with the added meaning of the sun having grown to full maturity, whereas the youthful sun, coming into being, is called Khepri, symbolized by the scarab hieroglyph. Atum, who has existed since all eternity, creates a divine couple: Shu, the air, and Tefnut, humidity, who, in turn, procreate another couple : Geb, the earth, and Nut, the sky. Two other couples spring from their union : Osiris and Isis, Seth and Nephthys. These primeval deities together formed a ninefold group called the divine *Ennead*. At this point begins the myth of Osiris in a host of different versions which make a coherent story almost impossible. The importance of these legends is tremendous: not only have they laid the foundations for all the popular beliefs, they have also inspired the daily rites in the temples, the cult of the dead and various superstitions or incantations. Osiris was a good king, who, according to Plutarch, had taught his people agriculture, arts and sciences. The wicked Seth, jealous of his brother's popularity, ordered his murder and the scattering of his dismembered body to the four winds. Isis and Nephthys, his sisters, seeking and finding the dispersed parts of Osiris' corpse, called in the help of their mother Nut and Anubis, son of Nephthys. Together they embalmed Osiris, whose mummy could still fecundate Isis. She gave birth to Horus, whom she hid away and brought up in the marshes of the Nile delta. Later on, this posthumous son of Osiris would avenge his father by gaining victory over his uncle Seth in a hand-to-hand fight. The gods reinstated Horus as ruler over Egypt and damned Seth. Osiris, for his part, ascended to heaven where he would, from that time onward, preside as judge over the dead. Every future Pharaoh will stress his hereditary kinship to Horus, whose name he incorporates into his titles, "Horus so and so" meaning "King so and so". Upon his death, the Pharaoh will become an Osiris, whose name, on the analogy of the previous, will stand for the "deceased so and so".

Had the Egyptian pantheon remained limited to the members of the *Ennead*, our task would have been a simple one. But there are numerous other deities. Nevertheless, these various deities do have certain characteristics in common. Originally the subject of local worship only, each of these deities gradually achieves the rank and status of supreme god, to the extent that they become assimilated to the master of the universe. Since this process was concluded before the beginning of the historical period, all these gods and goddesses are mentioned in the inscriptions as "masters" or "mistresses of the sky". A second characteristic of Egyptian gods is that they are generally grouped into triads, according to the formula father, mother and son. Finally, this very syncretism sometimes makes it difficult to distinguish between the specific functions or attributes of this or that deity. Nonetheless, the iconography, and the representation of the

hairdressings specifically, illustrates many of these distinctions much more clearly; it is also common knowledge that certain deities, although anthropomorphous, bear the head of the animal which has been consecrated to them.

The Egyptian conceptions of the underworld, on the other hand, are abundantly documented. The Egyptians themselves have written statements on the subject which, nevertheless, exact from us a twofold effort, one on the level of interpretation and one on the level of imagination, the risks of which can be assessed easily. The oldest of these texts are conventionally called *Pyramid Texts*, treating mainly of the Old Kingdom. For the Middle Kingdom, we have the so-called *Coffin Texts*. For the New Kingdom, which is our chief concern here, we dispose, first of all, of the well-known *Book of the Dead*, composed of 192 chapters and numerous vignettes. The exact title of this book is actually *Going out by Day* and tradition required that a copy of this book should be deposited next to the deceased and that - during the Ramesside period especially - passages from it should be copied onto the walls of the funeral chamber. The royal tombs also provide us with several "books" relating the wanderings of and the dangers encountered by the sun-god on his nocturnal journey. In his turn, the deceased king, son of Re, has to undertake the descent into the underworld. Three of these books are significant : the *Book of that which is in the underworld*, the *Book of the Gates* and the *Book of the Caverns*. Once again, text and images complement each other to draw a nightmare vision of the obstacles which have to be overcome in order to attain the kingdom of Osiris. Moreover the ground-plan of the tombs in the Valley of the Kings has been conceived in a way as to suggest a descent into the bowels of the earth. In the following pages, the first chapter gives a brief description of the Pharaoh's entry into the underworld, following in the footsteps of the sun-god Re, of whom he is both the son and the incarnation. The third chapter runs parallel to the first, but treats of the most humble of mortals. At this point we would like to expand slightly upon the eschatological visions the Egyptians might possibly have adhered to.

They held the belief that the deceased, like the setting sun, penetrated into the *Amentit*, the West, at the same time the underworld and the abode of the blissful. Having eliminated all obstacles with the assistance of the gods and the incantations from the *Book of the Dead*, the deceased arrived at the *Fields of Iaru*, the paradise of Osiris. A country not unlike Egypt, where grain and flax waxed high, with palm-trees and *dum*-palms and flowering shrubs, where a celestial river flowed, intersected by islands which could be reached by boat. There the deceased was given his own piece of land to cultivate, where he himself had to push the plough; the corn which he would harvest though, was of a celestial quality. It is true that, in order to be exonerated from this kind of labour, he could have recourse to some magical stratagem. He could store, in his tomb, 365 statuettes, one for each day of the year, which impersonated him and could carry out the daily tasks, requested by the gods, for him. These are the *ushabtis*, whose role it was to answer instead of the deceased when he was called upon. It was indeed considered one of the deceased's legitimate desires to rest and indulge in pleasures in the hereafter. The representations on the walls, whether painted or sculptured, now show the deceased seated with his wife, playing "chess", then again sitting at a table abundant with food or quenching his thirst at the celestial basin in the shadow of a *dum*-palm, because hunger and thirst were deemed impossible in the hereafter. This idea was sometimes symbolized by a superb sycamore tree, out of which emanated a goddess whose body fused with the trunk of the tree and who welcomed the deceased like a good fairy, offering them food and drink.

Still, this state of bliss could not be achieved without getting through an important event : the judgment of Osiris. Residing on the tribunal, the god of the dead was sitting enthroned under a canopy, like those of the Pharaohs. Next to him, standing upright, the goddesses Isis and Nephthys. Forty-two squatting deities attended the process. The deceased was then ushered in by Anubis, the god of embalmment, who led him before a balance. His heart, considered by the Egyptians as the seat of intelligence, was weighed in one of the scales, with either a feather or a figure representing Maat, the goddess of Truth and Justice, providing the counterbalance. Anubis inspected the "spring" of the balance, the god Thot inscribed the information on a writing board, while a monster, half-crocodile, half-hippopotamus, the Devourer of the Underworld, was hoping in vain to be awarded the heart of the deceased. Instead, the latter was proclaimed "justified" and led by Horus before Osiris, with whom he would become identified from that moment on.

In fact, if the deceased had been justified in this way, this was a result of the petition which he had submitted to Osiris upon his entrance into the *Hall of Justice* and which proclaimed his innocence : the well-known Chapter CXXV of the *Book of the Dead* which the Egyptologists generally term the *Declaration of Innocence*. Having recited this confession before the supreme judge, the deceased went on to read it before every one of the 42 deities of Osiris' tribunal, although with some modifications. The confession enumerated a list of vices and sins which the Egyptians disapproved of and, as such, and in spite of the stereotype, it acquires moral value in our eyes. Here are some lines from it :

> *I have not committed injustice.*
> *I have not stolen.*
> *I have not killed anybody.*
> *I have not been insolent.*
> *I have not been disobedient.*
> *I have not killed sacred livestock.*
> *I have not spied.*
> *I have not boasted.*
> *I have not fornicated.*
> *I have not been a sodomite nor a child-abuser.*

> *I have not been hypocritical.*
> *I have not insulted.*
> *I have not blasphemed the king.*
> *I have not blasphemed God.*

It is obvious that minor offences are mentioned alongside more serious vices here. This was the text that had to be recited to the 42 assessors. The version destined for Osiris contained more or less the same list, shorter in a way, but completed with some other reprehensible acts :

> *I have not inflicted suffering.*
> *I have not caused weeping.*
> *I have not tampered with the spring of the balance.*
> *I have not taken the milk from the mouths of the children.*
> etc.

The Egyptians firmly believed in eternal life as the above clearly indicates. In representing the deceased before Osiris in the hereafter, however, did they actually believe that the person would be reborn as skin, flesh and bones before being judged? Or was it rather the spiritual aspect they were alluding to? They indeed professed that man was made up of a material body and of something which we have translated as the soul, the *ba*, which was not the only immaterial element, for that matter. There was the *akh* and, more importantly, the *ka*. It is very difficult to define clearly which notions could be affixed to each of these three words. The *akh*, represented in hieroglyphics as a crested ibis, would, with all proper reservation, stand for that divine part of man to which he will return after his death. Philologists describe its meaning as "spirit". The *ka*, two raised arms in Egyptian hieroglyphics, is more complex. It is at the same time a reflection of the body, which, according to Maspero, is its "double", a guardian demon born together with man and never leaving him, even when deceased, man's individual destiny and man's vitality. This is a spiritual principle, but one which can never be separated from the body; once the body is dead, the *ka* will require a new support, the deceased's statue, his body for eternity. The *ba* is the only notion which seems akin to our conception of the soul. It is visibly independent from the body and leads its own life. In the tombs and on the papyri it is represented as a human-headed bird (p. 124). It can be observed descending to or coming out of the burial chamber, hovering over or perched on the mummy, in brief, watching over the corpse. With its gift of metamorphosis, it can also restore the deceased's corpse to life or transform it. Hence the necessity of embalmment and the repeatedly expressed aspiration of becoming an Osiris, in other words, to be resuscitated like this god. Likewise the Egyptian's desire to behold the face of the sun, to mount into the solar bark and accompany Re on his double circuit, illustrate that he believed in a possible regeneration.

It is the *Book of the Dead* once more, and chapter XVII in particular, which reveals the syncretism between the heliopolitan cosmogony and the Osirian myth in an interesting way. Numerous vignettes, reproduced in abundance in the tombs of the Ramesside period, illustrate this chapter, the title of which already bears significance in its own right :

"Here begin the praises and glorifyings of coming out from and of going into the glorious underworld which is in the beautiful West, of coming out by day in all the forms of existence which please the deceased, of playing at 'draughts' and sitting in the hall, and coming forth as a living soul…".

And the vignette shows the deceased playing, alone or with his wife, at this game called *senet*, a prefiguration of our game of draughts or game of goose. Studying this part of the *Book of the Dead* proves an instructive pursuit, because it is the only chapter to actually contain a religious doctrine, an embryo of exegesis even. The text indeed comments upon each of the consecutive vignettes, the most seductive succession of which can be found in the tomb of Nefertari and in the fourth and final chapter of this book. A monologue recalls, by the mouth of the god Atum, the birth of the universe from the Nun. Atum proclaims himself the One and Only by his identification with Re, the supreme god, who has created himself. Then, he adds :

"I am Yesterday and I know Tomorrow. Yesterday is Osiris. Tomorrow is Re, the day when the enemies of the universal master are slain so that his son Horus may reign".

In the vignette, Yesterday and Tomorrow are represented as two lions, sitting back to back and supporting the horizon (p.120-121), while the solar disc rises from a valley, with the whole scene being dominated by the vault of heaven. Next appears

"the Great Phoenix, who dwells in Heliopolis, the guardian of the book of what is and what will be".

A mummy on his catafalque is being watched over by two falcons taking the place of the goddesses Isis and Nephthys. Sometimes the soul hovers over the mummy.

"It is Osiris. It is his corpse. What is and what will be are in his body. It is Eternity and Infinity : Eternity is the day, Infinity is the night."

By now, the deceased is supposed to have reached his new fatherland. He stands before the door with two knock-ers which the god Atum traverses on his way to the *Fields of Iaru*. Here he greets the gods who welcome him and claims that he has sided with Horus against Seth. The allusion to the fight between Horus and Seth is rendered by a symbolic image :

the *Ujat* eye (p.43), which is at the same time the eye of Horus, torn out by Seth and restituted afterwards to its master, and the eye of Re which, according to some, has turned wrathful against Seth. Since it is said that Horus, having regained his eye, piously offered it to his father Osiris to bring him back to life, the *Ujat* eye has become the ultimate symbol of offering. But it is also thanks to this eye that the deceased can behold Re. This notion, in turn, probably induced the next scene : a chest with canopic jars, containing the deceased's bowels and watched over by four deities, called the sons of Horus, whom the deceased invokes in order that they might destroy all the sinfulness within him. These four deities are the human-headed Imset, the baboon-headed Hapi, the jackal-headed Duamutef and the falcon-headed Kebehsenuf (p. 54 and 160, bottom). Having named them, the deceased expresses his hope to meet Re face to face at last, as Osiris once did. But gaining access to the solar bark is not an easy task. First the malicious demons and monsters have to be vanquished by the power of Re, itself represented as a cat who, by the foot of the *ished* tree of Heliopolis, cuts off the head of the serpent Apophis, enemy of the universal master (p. 130). After this episode, the deceased, often accompanied by his wife, finally disembarks at the city of Re.

Re appears in his double bark, that of the day and that of the night. In that of the morning he is Khepri, the youthful sun, coming into being, his head replaced or surmounted by a scarab, followed by two baboons lifting their arms to the sky in adoration. In the evening bark, he is Atum, the sun in full maturity, represented in a disc and protected by a terrifying lion and the serpent-goddess Wajet, here called mistress of the flame.

Some of the vignettes of Chapter XVII of the *Book of the Dead* described above will recur in the third chapter of this book, notably when the funeral chambers of Sennejem and Inherkha will be discussed.

The reader must necessarily interpret this attempted description of Egyptian beliefs with respect to the hereafter, as incomplete and, in places, must manifestly refer to it with caution. Then, perhaps, it will allow him to wander through the labyrinth of the enormously diversified and apparently inextricable images presented in this book with less anxiety. Before concluding this introduction, we must at all times bear in mind that, in order to "merit his paradise", an Egyptian was not only deemed to know what would happen in the underworld, he would have to live the life of a pious citizen on earth as well, worshipping the gods (especially the ones of the underworld), completing the pilgrimage to Abydos where, according to one tradition, reposed the head of Osiris and, last but not least, undergoing the required funeral rites - embalmment and opening of the mouth in particular - upon which the second chapter will touch briefly.

CHAPTER I

BIBAN EL-MULUK
Valley of the Kings

ny conversation about Egypt immediately conjures up the image of the pyramids, those tombs of the powerful - or at least deemed so - Pharaohs of the Old Kingdom. In fact, these monuments symbolize the passage to Eternity by their very nature. Pyramids, in a way, represent the crystallization of sun-rays. As the king, the son of the sun, i.e. the earthly incarnation of the god, is buried in the pyramid, he becomes one with his heavenly father and so reaches the underworld. From the Vth Dynasty onwards, hieroglyphic inscriptions around the burial chamber, which we call "pyramid texts", remind us of the fact that the Pharaoh, on his celestial journey, encounters various divinities, eventually and according to the time of day, turning them into his daily meal. This chapter has been surnamed the *Theophagy*, underlining the idea that the deceased king is unified with the gods by absorbing everyone of them. The "fashion" of building pyramids as royal tombs originates with the IIIrd Dynasty - although the first one, built for King Djoser on a rectangular ground-plan, can only be partly called so - and continues up to the end of the Middle Kingdom, initially in the immense necropolis of Memphis, currently embracing the region between Abu Roash and Meidum, later in the region of the Fayum. Nevertheless, by the XIth Dynasty, and thanks to the efforts of the Mentuhoteps, Thebes became the kingdom's capital as well as the place where the Pharaohs ordered their mortal remains to be buried, at the foot of the Deir el-Bahari cliffs to be more exact.

The modern city of Luxor is the site of ancient Thebes. In fact, its surface extended over both banks of the Nile; the City of the Living, where the majestic ruins of the temples of the god Amun in Karnak and in Luxor itself, still exist, is situated to the East, whilst the City of the Dead, virtually unique in its kind in the world, is located on the West bank. Having developed into the capital of an Empire, especially since the XVIIIth Dynasty, Thebes, or *Waset* in Egyptian, was more often referred to as *niout*, a word which means *The City* and no small indication of its enormous prestige. The Bible will mention it as *No* or *No Amon, City of Amun*. Homer, on the other hand, uses the epithet *Thebes-with-the-Hundred-Gates*, an allusion, undoubtedly, to the numerous temple pylons which could be seen there. Even after the Egyptian capital had shifted to the Delta, Thebes remained an important locality until the Graeco-Roman period.

The Theban Necropolis covers a vast area, extending itself beyond the cultivated zone for many kilometres. The royal and princely tombs are grouped into two *wadis*: the Valley of the Kings, up North, and the Valley of the Queens, in the South. The graves of other individuals - dignitaries, nobles or plain mortals - were brought together into several sectors, all of which now carry Arabic names, derived, notably, from existing villages inhabited by local peasants : Dira' Abul-Naga, Khokha, 'Assassif, Sheikh abdel-Gurna, Gurnet Mar 'i, Deir el-Medina. During the New Kingdom, each Pharaoh had his own funeral temple built, but most of these have since been destroyed or now lie in ruins. Only those of Sethos I in Gurna, of Queen Hatshepsut and Thutmosis III in Deir el-Bahari, of Ramesses II called the Ramesseum and of Ramesses III in Medinet Habu have survived. As for the colossi of Memnon, they are the only relics of a giant temple erected by Amenophis III who, furthermore, ordered the construction of a palace in the outermost Southern part of the Necropolis, in a place called Malqata. Beyond that point there only subsists a small temple, dedicated to the goddess Isis, but it dates from the Roman period.

The Valley of the Kings, *Biban el-Muluk* in Arabic, occupies a first rank place in this ensemble, both by the impressing outlook of the rock-tombs excavated there, as by the interest sparked off by the infernal scenes within. These scenes cover the walls of their long corridors and, sometimes, the ceiling of the burial chamber, called *golden hall*, whereas the ceilings of the descending corridors are decorated either with stars or with vultures symbolizing the sky goddess. In reality, there are two valleys, the more Westward one only being visited by very few Egyptologists. The main valley resembles a gigantic funnel eroded from the desert plateau by heavy, antediluvian rainfall and from which a meandering *wadi* searches its way towards the plain. This is where the kings from the XVIIIth up to the XXth Dynasty have been buried, from between 1550 to 1100 B.C.. Having inaugurated this cycle, Amenophis I with his mother, Queen Ahmes-Nefertari, was later to be hailed as the *patron saint* of the Theban Necropolis, so to speak. There are some sixty-odd tombs. The importance ascribed to each of them naturally depends on their state of preservation and their size. Among the most frequented tombs we find, in chronological order, those of Thutmosis III (1501-1448 B.C.), situated in a deep ravine, Amenophis II (1448-1422 B.C.), at the foot of an abrupt cliff, Tutankhamun (1358-1350 B.C.), famous for the discovery of his treasure, Haremhab (1347-1314 B.C.), the general who became king, Ramesses I (1314-1312 B.C.), founder of the XIXth Dynasty, Sethos I (1312-1298 B.C.), one of the, if not the most spectacular tomb, Merenptah (1225-1215 B.C.), the Pharaoh of the Exodus, Ramesses III (1193-1166 B.C.), Ramesses VI, whose tomb preserved the grave of Tutankhamun and Ramesses IX, both of whom can be situated, with the last of the Ramessides, in the second half of the 12th century B.C. Describing each grave separately would prove an unavailing task. Useful details abound in scientific publications and tourist guides written by specialists. We will confine ourselves to point out some of the peculiarities which are characteristic of certain tombs. Before we do that, however, a brief general introduction, intended to explain some of the iconography common to most of the royal tombs, might be useful.

The principle is to enable the sovereign of Egypt, son of the gods, to travel safely through the twelve hours of night in the company of the god Re, represented as a man with a ram's head, wearing a solar disc (p. 38, 74...) and navigating into the underworld. Theologians of the Pharaonic period have written many a book elaborating this idea concretely, books to which artists have contributed significant illustration material. The most important of these books is known as the *Book of that which is in the underworld*. The notion of Egyptian hell is, up to a certain point, conceived quite similarly to that of the land of the living. Having shed his light onto the latter, the Sun-God penetrates obscurity and, conducting his bark on an underground river, travels from region to region, twelve in all, to bring light to the inhabitants of what the texts call the *Amduat*. Nevertheless he has to defeat the ambushes laid by his enemies and overcome the obstacles put in his way by his most feared foe, the mighty and wicked serpent Apophis. In picturing this infernal world, ancient Egyptians have certainly given free expression to their imagination. In a second volume, entitled *The Book of the Gates* they describe twelve portals which are protected by fire-spitting serpents. For a change, these creatures show a favourable attitude towards Re, so the god can progress without difficulty. Still other books complete this vision of the sun's nocturnal journey. The book entitled *Book of the qererts or caverns* alludes to the deceased deities' cemetery,

where they rest in their respective sarcophagi. As for the vaulted ceiling of the burial chamber, it is usually painted in yellow on a black background: the sky goddess Nut, a stretched-out woman whose naked and starry body somehow constitutes a vault, swallows the sun in the evening and gives birth to it twelve hours later (p. 64-65). This scene, which assumes enormous proportions, may occur twice, once symbolizing the sky by day and, conversely, picturing it at night. Such a representation in the tomb of Sethos I, the ceiling of which has collapsed recently, had been ornamented with interesting astronomical designs : constellations, signs of the zodiac, etc.

From a stylistic point of view, the royal tombs tend to differ. They are quintessential in painting a lively picture of the evolution of Egyptian art, eliminating, in the process, any possible misconceptions about its seemingly immobile sameness : every period nurtures its proper aesthetical values. The tombs of Thutmosis III and of his son and successor, Amenophis II, for instance, display linear, almost sketchy drawings which would verge on the simplistic, if it weren't for the remarkable dexterity and expressive power with which they were outlined. With a mere stroke the artist succeeds in conveying movement to his figures, drawn in black or, occasionally, red on a yellow background, thus simulating a huge scroll of papyrus rolled out along the wall. The over-all impression created by this kind of succession of vignettes is quite astounding : the similarity to an animated cartoon is one of the first comparisons to spring to mind. The most striking example of this style can be found on a pillar of Thutmosis III's burial chamber : the King is suckled by the sycamore goddess, who is identified with Isis (p. 18, top). The sacred tree is delicately suggested by a few red strokes for the branches and some blue-green dots for the foliage. Out of the firm tree-trunk a human arm appears in support of a large female breast on which the tiny-looking Pharaoh figure flings himself to quench his thirst. The way in which he clings to the inferior line of the arm, far too heavy for his small hands, is of a rare poetic beauty.

The small tomb of Tutankhamun, once laden with so many treasures, is relatively poor from an iconographic view-point, yet the images of human greatness which cover the walls of the sarcophagus chamber still recall the Amarnian art of the reformer Amenophis IV - Akhenaten (1375-1358 B.C.). The king's funeral is followed by the ritual known as the ritual of *the opening of the mouth*, which is being performed by the old king Ay, successor to the young Tutankhamun, on his predecessor's body. After this ritual he is welcomed by the sky goddess Nut, and, afterwards, by the god Osiris. The West wall is entirely dedicated to an illustration hailing from the *Book of the Dead* and showing some baboons (p. 17).

With Haremhab and Ramesses I, we witness a return to the purer, more classical style of the XVIIIth Dynasty as if there had never been a stylistic rupture of any sort or as if the Theban artists had wilfully ignored the innovations introduced by the revolutionary predecessor of the unfortunate Tutankhamun. The continuity between the reigns of Haremhab and Ramesses I, both really army officers clothed with royal power, is so fluent that photographs of either tomb might indeed be confounded quite easily. The painted bas-reliefs have retained all of their freshness. The fact that the work on Haremhab's tomb never saw completion, allows a close examination of the successive phases of execution (p. 28-29) : the preparation of the wall, an initial drawing in red ink and subsequent corrections in black, the rough cutting of the stone, some finished details, not yet heightened with paint, and, in the sarcophagus hall, hieroglyphics on the corner walls to allow the decorators to orientate themselves when they had to adjudge the correct wall to the religious scenes, following rigorous traditional guide-lines. In some places, everything appears so clean that it seems as if the artisans have only left for a short while and might be expected back any minute to take up their unachieved work again. The knowledge that a lapse of 3300 years can be wiped out so incredibly abruptly is one of the most shaking experiences on such a visit.

With the exception of one unfinished room, with walls only containing some large preparatory drawings, and even these being traced out with unspeakable virtuosity, the sculptured and painted tomb of Sethos I rightly stands as the showpiece of the Valley of the Kings. Unfortunately the growing number of tourist visits over the last few years and the inevitable consequences - with dust and pollution causing damages not unlike those of the Lascaux caverns - have incited the responsible authorities to prohibit further access to the tomb. In addition, the collapse of the vaulted ceiling of the sepulchral chamber involves a considerable risk for visitors who may not have the opportunity now to view this marvellous tomb for a long time to come. Consolation, in the mean time, can still be found in a visit to Abydos, where the reliefs in the same king's temple, bear testament to an unequalled perfection.

There is no representation, within this volume, of the tomb of Merenptah, which, though substantially damaged, has been mentioned above for the simple reason that it should be visited in pursuit of that elusive emotion, that indescribable leap of the heart only felt when, at the end of a long descent, one comes face to face with the lid of a colossal sarcophagus, sculptured in granite and showing the features of the dead Pharaoh, resting recumbent and with crossed arms, in eternal peace.

The XXth Dynasty ushers in the decadence of Pharaonic art. Of this period three tombs attract the most visitors mainly because of their state of preservation and their accessibility: Ramesses III, Ramesses VI and Ramesses IX. Ramesses III's tomb is astonishing because of the ten small chambers excavated on either side of the entrance corridor and serving, probably, as stores for the objects depicted on the walls : kitchen implements, ship's models, *uraei*, weapons, vases,

elephant's tusks, necklaces, furniture, oars, harps, etc. In the tombs of Ramesses VI and Ramesses IX we should direct some special attention towards the above-mentioned scenes of the infernal world, as well as to the double representation of the diurnal and nocturnal sky-goddess on the vaulted ceiling of the burial chamber. Finally, a passing reference should be made to the tomb of Ramesses IV, on the fact that it was inhabited by Coptic monks some fifteen centuries later, as the Christian scenes, superimposed on the images of pagan Egypt, illustrate : **sic transit gloria mundi**.

Cartouche with the name
of King Haremhab

CHAPTER II

SHEIKH ABDEL-GURNA
The Nobles' Tombs

ituated almost centrally in the Necropolis lies the village of Sheikh abdel-Gurna, incorporating some of the most beautiful Theban tombs. Not the resting-place of kings or princes of the royal family, but of high-ranked dignitaries of the court, of administration, clergy and army, which is why these tombs are usually denoted as the private tombs or tombs of the nobles. Some 450 of these, dispersed over the six areas mentioned earlier, have currently been identified. Just how many exactly belong to the area under discussion, is hard to say, although it would seem a fair supposition to say around 150. There is no strict numbering system; numbers have been allocated as new discoveries were being made. These numbers now allow us to distinguish between various individuals who sometimes shared identical names, but belonged to different periods. A common usage, in that respect, is the incorporation between brackets of these reference numbers whenever mention is made of a particular name.

Properly speaking, these tombs are funeral chapels, dug out from the flank or at the foot of the hills. Some are sculptured, others painted. All have been conceived following a more or less uniform scheme, allowing nonetheless for quite a number of variations. The basic model looks something like this : a small, outdoor court leads onto a door of a room which is broader than it is deep, followed, in turn, by a second, long and narrow chamber, which is arranged perpendicularly to it. At the furthest extremity of this chamber there is a niche destined to hold the deceased's statue. The ground-plan of this kind of tomb resembles an inverted *T*. A deep pit or a descending corridor leads down to the burial chamber, where the presently removed sarcophagus and the funeral furniture once used to rest. The sepulchral room itself was rarely decorated, with the possible exception of funerary texts every now and then. The burial vault of Sennufer (96), mayor of Thebes under the reign of Amenophis II, however, belies this general rule completely. The chapel in itself, considered by the Egyptians to be the deceased's eternal dwelling, should reflect, on its walls, the most diverse and attractive aspects of life on earth on the one hand, but also, in order to perpetuate them, the rituals with which the deceased has been buried, on the other. To enumerate all the themes treated by Egyptian artists appears a wearisome task. Such enumerations make up the contents of many a specialized work, or, at least, of less concise publications than this volume. Reference can be made, for one, to the book on Egyptian Painting published by one of the authors of the present and a large source of inspiration to it.

Upon entering a well-preserved Theban tomb, one is struck as much by the freshness of the colours as by the multitude of painted figures, crowding on the walls, one above or next to the other in one of the many different registers, together forming an unending procession. Generally speaking, the artist paints his scene in a rectangle or square which he inserts in a register with a height varying between 30 and 40 cm. To comply with the Pharaonic spirit, every scene, every single figure at that, must needs be isolated and analyzed in its own right, without looking for what we, today, might label "the context". Some archaeologists have stated that Egyptian artists tended to represent things rather in a cerebral than in a realistic manner, and that, consequently, the images and scenes on the walls of temples and tombs should be interpreted as another, "enlarged" way of writing. The theory opposing this thesis, in that case, would seem the more plausible one : for centuries on end, the sense of decoration and love of simple, almost mathematical, composition of the Egyptian scribe allowed him to maintain a hieroglyphic script of a nature so ornamental that it could often rival pictorial master-works with great ease.

The Theban mountain is a calcarean massif, although the limestone is not of the same quality everywhere. Only a few select and powerful individuals, such as Ramose (55), vizier and governor of Thebes, and Khaemhet (57), royal scribe and inspector of the granaries of Upper and Lower Egypt under the reign of Amenophis III (1411-1375 B.C.), could indulge in the luxury of having their tombs decorated with magnificently sculptured bas-reliefs which, moreover, were to be heightened with paint like the scenes which adorn the temple-walls and royal tombs. The rock structure permitting, the stone-mason carefully smoothed out the walls, filling up cracks and crevices with coarse-grained plaster wherever necessary, enabling the painter to apply his preparation directly onto the stone. A paramount example of this type of tomb is that of Userhet (56), a scribe who had been brought up in the royal nursery, together with Amenophis II (1448-1422 B.C.).

For the majority of paintings at Sheikh abdel-Gurna, however, stucco, and not stone, provided the required support. On the rock-face's rough surface a thick layer of mud plaster was applied, visibly in several goings, the wet loam being mixed with straw to ensure consistency. On top of this mud wall another thin film, composed of plaster and finely ground stone, was applied to a thickness of about 2 mm. A smooth mortar "canvas" like this reflected even the subtlest of strokes! Depending on its particular structure the stucco, generally of a grimy colour, only yielded shades ranging from grey to beige and brown. It did not act a ground to the pictures, but had to be given a coat of paint, most commonly with the pearl-grey colour favoured in the XVIIIth Dynasty. Still, this did not prevent artists later on - through negligence or plain haste? - from applying the paint directly onto the mud wall, having treated it only with the merest hint of white paint. The frailty of such works of art can hardly be underestimated, considering the imminent threat of flaking and being turned to dust. It is a miracle that they have resisted the ravages of time as it is. Close examination confirms our anxious suspicions as to what might happen if even the slightest breath of air disturbed the dried-up earthen wall with its fragile, membranous layers of paint. Experience has illustrated the risks involved in the imprudent handling of these paintings. Wiping away the dust from certain scenes in order to photograph them, or trying to remove a spider's web from the corner of a painted wall, might seem harmless enough, but, more often than not, cause irreparable damage through the removal of bits of paint.

The Pharaonic painter's palette is very simple and his technique is known as the *tempera* process. The pigments were readily available in nature, fit to be ground into powder and diluted with a mixture of water and gum to ensure their adherence to the wall. Ochrous colours seemed to prevail: red, yellow and brown, each providing the artist with a range of shades with varying intensity, depending on the degree of dilution. They were generally used to represent the human flesh. Whitewash came in second and was mainly used for garments : one or several superposed layers could create an impression of transparency or opacity, as the artist intended. Mixed with or applied over red, it proved perfect for the tender pink colour of the female complexion and of specific fruits, animals or items of food which can usually be seen in offering scenes. Blue and green were quite common colours

as well and they derived from a copper frit. Because of their joint origin, it is sometimes difficult to distinguish between them. Blue on a white background counterfeited the subtle and transparent shades of the zigzagging water ideally. Green, on the other hand, was reserved for the foliage of trees or thickets of papyrus, for offerings of vegetables or flowers and for specific components of jewellery (necklaces, bracelets, girdles...), where it simulated the effect of enameled earthenware beads. It is also the colour most liable to alter after it has been exposed to air, sometimes turning into a reddish, rusty colour, sometimes even disintegrating altogether, or, worse still, affecting the underlying layer of stucco and dragging down entire areas of the painting in its fall. Black is possibly even more transitory. Composed of soot, it hardly stuck to the wall as the other colours. This is one of the reasons why the large wigs of some of the ladies seem to have disappeared, uncovering the yellowish background of limestone or stucco - notably in the tomb of Userhet (56). Unaware of this peculiarity, one might almost be induced to believe that Egyptian women of the New Kingdom were blondes! In mixtures, however, black seems to have proven more consistent. The grey colour, obtained by mixing black with white, was very suitable for birds or the pleated dresses of mourning women. Mixed with ochre, black served to accentuate the red colour. These colours were applied in flat tints and their choice could either be conventional or arbitrary. Properly arranged, they could be used to stunning decorative effect.

The Necropolis of Sheikh abdel-Gurna is one of the world's most delightful art galleries in its own right. Unfortunately, the few images illustrating this chapter cannot nearly serve to give an adequate idea of the riches contained therein. On the top of the hill, for instance, stands the large tomb of Antefoker (60), governor of the city and vizier under the reign of Sesostris I (ca 1950 B.C.), characteristic of the slightly rigid style of the Middle Kingdom, otherwise barely represented in Thebes.

Naturally, this particular area of the ancient Thebans' burial-grounds serves best of all to study the New Kingdom (from about 1500 to 1100 B.C.). Schematically speaking, the evolution of Egyptian art since the beginning of the XVIIth Dynasty until the Ramesside period, can be categorized into five easily recognizable phases. With the first *Thutmosides* (first half of the 15th century B.C.), numerous affinities with the Middle Kingdom continue to exist : a certain severity of outlook and slight stiffness of movement, a love of symmetrical compositions and the use of conspicuous and opaque colours on a sky-blue background. Under Amenophis II (1448-1422 B.C.) and Thutmosis IV (1422-1411 B.C.), the movements gain suppleness and grace, the scenes are composed with more liberty and fantasy, colours appear in a wider range of shades, lighter, sometimes verging on the transparent, while the background usually consists of neutral, grey-blue colours. The synthesis of the preceding periods comes with the reign of Amenophis III (1411-1375

B.C.). The purity of the finest works can best be termed classical, inspired by soberness and reserve. This delicacy is also apparent from the choice and richness of the shades palette, providing a better harmony with the white colour, which is now becoming increasingly important as background colour. The reign of Amenophis IV - Akhenaten (1375-1358 B.C.) leaves a hiatus, followed by a short transition period, that of Tutankhamun (1358-1350 B.C.). On the other hand, the passage from the XVIIIth to the XIXth Dynasty (grosso modo the second half of the 14th century B.C.) is characterized by two tendencies : one reactionary, consequently of an academical nature, the other progressive in a way foreboding the picturesque style of certain Ramesside painters. The epoch of the Ramesses, which stretches over a long period of time (13th and 12th centuries B.C.), is usually frowned upon as a harbinger of decadence. The best works are often marked by virtuosity and negligence alike. These, however, will be scrutinized in the next two chapters.

This brief, and purely theoretical, outline might have benefited from some factual back-up by the introduction of some illustrations, but that is a concept which other publications have attempted and achieved successfully before us and, furthermore, it lies not inside the scope of this book to do so: the very title of our publication forbids it. On the other hand, this does not prevent us from touching briefly upon some of the scenes which form part of these tombs' iconography. Day-to-day life seems to be one of the major preoccupations here. There are, so to speak, no biographical reminiscences - although these are not absent altogether - but what it all boils down to in the end is the representation of an ideal life. Agriculture, the growing of grain and flax, the vineyard and the wine-press, hunting in the desert and fowling in the marshes, fishing and crafts all seem to work together towards the same goal : assuring that the deceased can enjoy the same luxuries in the underworld as in his mortal life, food and drink, clothing and finery, furniture, etc. Persons holding some high office during their life-time, who perhaps even met their sovereign in the flesh, reproduce the latter's portrait in their "home of eternity". Thus the Pharaoh can occasionally be seen welcoming his foreign tributaries, who are bringing him samples of their countries' produce. Or he might be inspecting his army, composed of both indigenous troops and Libyan or African mercenaries. Scenes in which the Pharaoh is attending some or other religious ceremony are of rare occurence. Rekhmire (100), governor of Thebes and vizier under Thutmosis III and Amenophis II, receives the king's instructions, a text covering an entire wall and revealing the moral qualities the minister has to live up to. Not a square inch of the enormously high walls of the two rooms of this tomb has been left uncovered. An inconceivable number of painted scenes sketch a summary of all the activities of the Theban community which have been carried out under the vizier's leadership. Because his funeral chapel is at present inaccessible, we can only visit the burial chamber of Sennufer (96), another mayor of Thebes under Amenophis II. This room, however, is unique of its sort.

An ostensibly major figure at Amenophis II's court (1448-1422 B.C.), the royal scribe Userhet, if we may take his word for it, directed the provisioning and perhaps even the enlistment of the soldiers. Before the enthroned Pharaoh on one of the first room's walls, we can indeed see the young recruits arriving at the gate of the barracks, where they are arrayed in a tight order, squatting in front of their individual, well-filled basket of victuals (p. 79). The Egyptian army staff believed in well-groomed and catered for troops. In evidence, and right underneath, we encounter the well-known barbers' scene (p. 78). Traditionally, barbers in the Orient have no saloon and they carry out their grooming tasks in open air. The inherent humour of the scene is enhanced by the painter's representation of his figures as Chinese silhouettes, in red ochre, broken only by the white colour of the loin-cloths. We may even distinguish a Negroid character. The figures are in fact boys having, or about to have, their head shaved. Two of them are between the barbers' hands right now. The others are patiently awaiting their turn, cowering on the ground or sitting on a small stool. Some are engaged in a brisk, mimic conversation, whilst others are dozing off in the shadow of a tree. One client has found and egoistically laid claim to a folding chair, leaving his comrade to sit virtually on the edge. The whole painting genuinely breathes real life. In the second chamber, Userhet, adopting his sovereign's fondness of sporting achievements, is shown standing upright on a chariot and launching himself into a desert hunting party with great energy. The scene has been conceived in the grand manner. Two galloping horses, one red, the other white, pull the light chariot on which stands Userhet, reins wound around his body to direct the animals with simple, well-considered movements. This leaves his hands free to manipulate bow and arrow against wild animals. The latter are scattering, wounded and panting : antelopes and hyenas have been caught up in an inextricable tangle. The artist who created this piece was an animal-lover beyond doubt : he has actually succeeded in humanizing their suffering. Two details are particularly moving in that respect. Below the horses' bellies, we see an arrow-stricken hare leaping over the body of a tortured hyena, its tongue sticking out as it slowly dies. The agility of the hare put to flight is well-rendered by some red strokes defining the contours of the animal's brownish yellow body. The same freshness of inspiration can also be witnessed in another detail of this hunting scene, the sensibility of which is so pure that it still shouts out its message after thousands of years : a fox, huddled up to a bush, is slowly agonizing. Its paws pressed against the supporting shrub, its crooked back, its haggard look, all combine to express fear and astonishment at such misfortune. The contrast between the general agitation of the scene above and the silent tragedy which unfolds in a small corner, is quite significant. The ability to render this drama without grandiloquence or high-flown lyricism, by applying a mere red point to a white blot for the eye of the animal, requires prodigious insight. Only rarely has artistic genius achieved this degree of constraint, saying so much in so little words. Stripped of all artifice, this work of art, whilst setting out from a wretched subject, attains sublimity. Nothing spectacular, yet a pure gem.

Khaemhet (57), inspector of the royal granaries under Amenophis III, ordered two sculptures of the king, superbly seated on his throne (though the heads, sadly enough, have been removed and are currently on display at the Berlin Museum) : he receives the homages of his subjects. Some of the episodes of the deceased's career are also described. The second, ransacked chamber, was reserved to funeral themes. Three fragments of this tomb's bas-reliefs have ended up at the Brussels museum. Ramose (55), on the other hand, governor and vizier during Amenophis IV's reign and principal of the most beautiful sculptured tomb come down to us, is shown receiving golden necklaces from the hands of the Pharaoh, either as a reward or decoration. There is also a life-size representation of Ramose standing upright and holding the symbolic key to the city. An entire wall is dedicated to the representation of seated couples, supposedly family members : the fine craftsmanship of the engraving, bringing to mind the art of medallion-making, is a feast for the eyes.

One may well imagine that the Egyptians also drew plenty of inspiration from death, as opposed to the scenes they derived from life on earth, as those just discussed. The different phases of the funeral ritual seemed especially appealing to the artist. Summarizing, we might indicate the discrete suggestion of the embalmment, hardly ever more than by some gestures of purification, with the person quite often still represented as being alive. In order to ascertain the favourable disposition of the ruler of the underworld, it was every Egyptian's wish to have made a pilgrimage to the principal sanctuary of Osiris, at Abydos. In case this wish had not been realized during one's life-time, there was at least still the possibility of undertaking the voyage after one's death, and before being put to the grave. This explains why so many Theban paintings show the mummified bodies of the deceased and his wife, placed on a boat descending the Nile with the help of oars and, afterwards, ascending it again with all sails set, propelled by the North wind (p. 82). Once this sacred duty fulfilled, the actual funeral rites may begin, or the transfer of the body from the right bank to the left bank of Thebes, to be more precise. Several flat-bottomed vessels transport the funeral cortege. At the head of the procession sails a bark which is taking the one with the catafalque in tow. Other vessels follow, carrying priests, mourners, family members and friends, funeral furniture and offerings. Having disembarked on the opposite river bank, the cortege occasionally has to follow heavy tracks to arrive at the site of the tomb. The procession continues this way until it reaches a court arranged in the mountain-side with an entrance to the rock-tomb. In front of the tomb's door, the coffin and a statue of the deceased, his so-called *ka*, deemed to be his eternal body from now on, have been erected. The priest who directs the funeral rites is called *sem* (p. 80, bottom). Dressed in a leopard's skin, he carries out a rite known as *the opening of the mouth* (p. 122, top). With a hooked-like device and some silex instruments he performs the gesture of opening the organs of the senses, after which he presents the statue with the foreleg of a freshly sacrificed calf or ox. Then ensues the moving moment when the mummy, who has been reanimated for eternity, is finally commended to the tomb. In reality, this involved it being sunk down to the bottom of a 10 m deep pit. With the deceased now peacefully resting in the silence of the burial chamber, one final ceremony has to be completed before the cortege leaves the cemetery : the consecration of the offerings by the priest of the *ka*, a rite which, this time, is carried out at the end of the second chamber, in front of the shrine where the statue, support of the *ka*, will replace the deceased. The frequent representations of banquets in these tombs would suggest a funeral meal near the tomb as a symbol of communion with the deceased, before the party dispersed or returned to the city. There are even suppositions that such meals may have recurred at more or less regular intervals after the funeral.

As regards our knowledge of funeral rites, Sennufer's tomb (96) proves vitally important. It is quite certain that, once the access to the steep staircase had been bricked up, no one ever set foot into the tomb again, a principle which should be strongly recommended once more. The ever-increasing number of visitors indeed pollutes the air in the tomb continually and without a chance of renewal. The dust, kicked up from unabatedly trampled upon floors, sticks to the painted walls. The candles or oil lamps which are lighted whenever there is an electricity breakdown, inflict irreparable damage to the beautiful colours. That is perhaps why the Kodak company has realized a remarkable photographic facsimile of the tomb, which has thus far been exhibited in three German cities - Köln, Hildesheim and Berlin - and in Linz, in Austria. This subterranean chamber, with its four pillars and badly squared walls and ceiling, is exclusively decorated with scenes of a religious nature, some painted on the walls, the others onto the four faces of the square pillars, but all, as usual, without any logical order : mummification and purification of the body, pilgrimage to Abydos, opening of the mouth and libation of the deceased and his wife, worship of the gods of the underworld, Osiris and Anubis, coming out by day or, in other words, resurrection. Of course there are also the bringers of offerings and the sacrifice of animals. We are witness to the touching gestures of tenderness exchanged between man and wife, and, once only, the symbolic meeting with the goddess of the sycamore tree, represented as a fairy-like apparition between the foliage, the whole only being a fictitious subject, since it is but a wooden pole which had to be carried along in religious processions. The most striking aspect of this tomb, however, is the decoration of the rough ceiling, covered by an immense vineyard conjuring up the illusion of a natural landscape. Is this merely an ornamental scene or does it carry symbolic weight? Nobody, until now, seems to have resolved this enigma. In spite of their attractiveness, the paintings of Sennufer's tomb (96) suddenly appear coarse when com-

(continued on page 177)

CHAPTER I

BIBAN EL MULUK

THE VALLEY OF THE KINGS

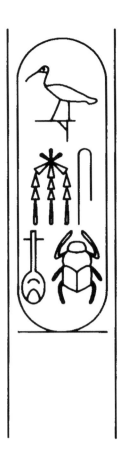

THUTMOSIS IIII

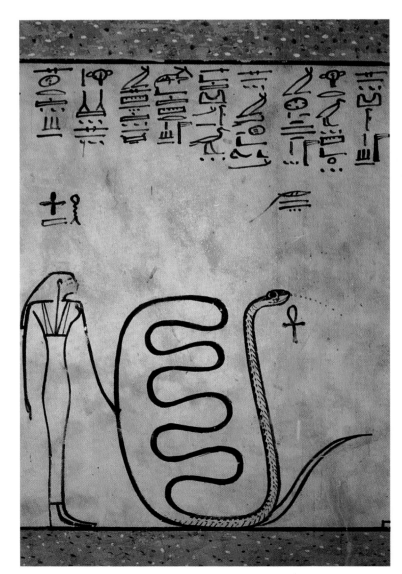

19

Thutmosis III suckling Isis' breast, represented as goddess of the sycamore-tree. *(p. 18, top)*

Eighth hour of the Amduat. The god Hunet, the goddess Mehen-ta and a large snake with curling tail. *(p. 18, bottom right)*

First hour of the Amduat. Three of the nine baboons welcoming the sun-god entering into the Amduat, themselves preceded by twelve serpents. *(p. 18, bottom left)*

◁

Tenth hour of the Amduat. Two crowned divinities are facing the crowned, two-headed and four-legged snake *tshesu-heru.* The black hawk on the snake represents the soul of the god Sokar. *(p. 19, top)*

The sun-god passes through the secret caverns of *Sokar.* In these dangerous caverns, falcon-headed *Sokar* is parting the wings of a three-headed serpent. *(p. 19, bottom)*

▷

An inscription in simplified hieroglyphics.

▽

First hour of the Amduat. Three serpents, preceded by three deities, in front of a bark which contains Kheper.

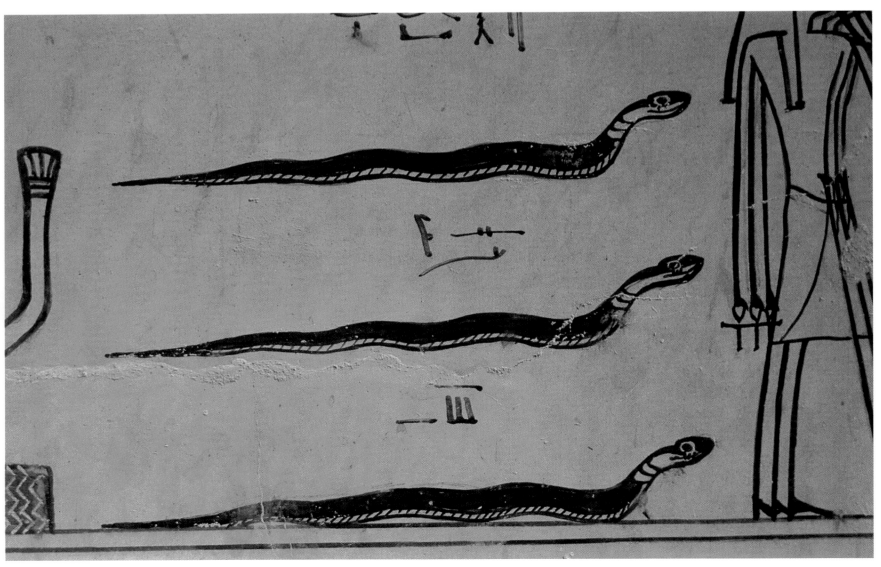

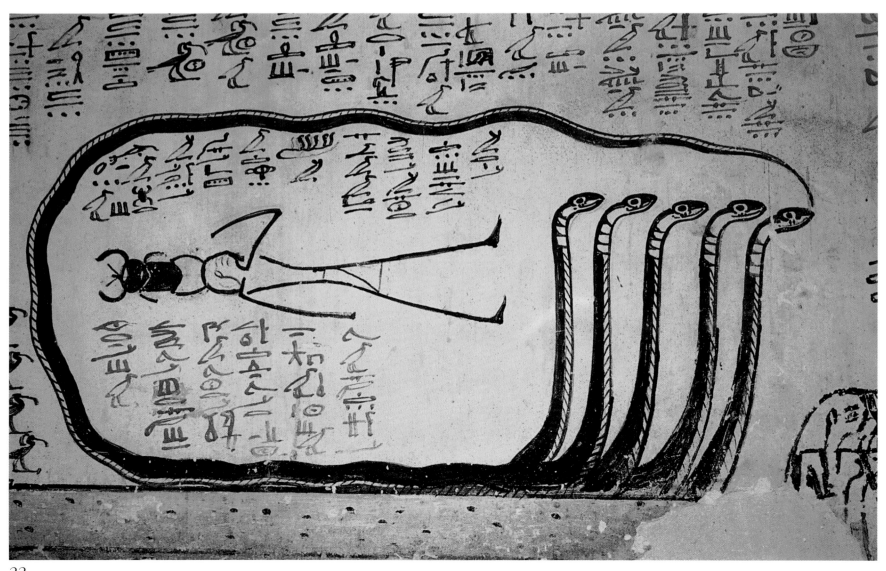

Seventh hour of the Amduat. The enthroned god Shepes, the lion-headed goddess Hekenet and the human-headed serpent Ankhet are preceded by Osiris who is coiled and protected by Ankh-Iru, one of the shapes of the serpent Mehen.

The five-headed snake Asha-heru is coiling an upright man with a scarab on his head, symbolizing Khepri's body.

Twelfth Hour of the Amduat. (Detail) The scarab Kheper, the air-god Shu and the solar disc penetrating into the horizon.

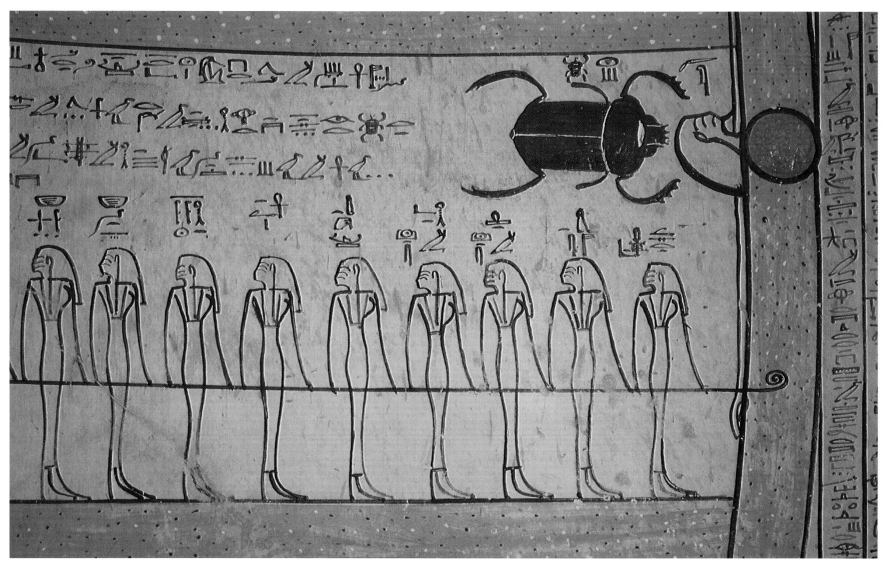

Third hour of the Amduat. Various deities
sailing in the underworld.

AMENOPHIS II

▽

Second hour of the Amduat. Deities, their heads decorated with corn in the ear.

26

The king offering wine to the goddess Hathor.

HAREMHAB

King Haremhab before the goddess Hathor,
Mistress of the West.

▽ ▷

Nefertum, son of the god Ptah of Memphis
and of the lion-headed goddess Sekhmet,
wearing a blue lotus flower which symbolizes
the fragrances he is the master of.

Third Hour of the Book of the Gates : the Sea of Fire. Twelve blissful souls with human heads. Before them, in the soil, ears of corn provided by the ambivalent sea who is salvation and damnation at the same time : refreshment for Osiris and the blissful, torment of fire for the damned sinners. In addition twelve mummies (three on the right) are represented as being protected by the serpent Sety. In the lower register, the bark of the earth. *(see also page 40-41)*

Haremhab's cartouches. In principle, the Pharaoh's most important names are surrounded by a cartouche : the throne name as king of Upper and Lower Egypt, and the birth name (nomen) introduced by the title "son of Re".

Osiris, mummified, god of vegetation and resurrection, is pictured with a green complexion, the colour of sprouting life and vegetation. Osiris is wearing the white crown with ostrich-feathers and holds the royal attributes as "ruler over the dead".

The goddess Hathor, mistress of the West.

The goddess Isis receiving two bowls of wine from the king.

Haremhab worshipping Hathor, goddess of
the West, who is wearing a black wig, and
offering wine to Horus. At the extreme right
stands the goddess Isis.

34

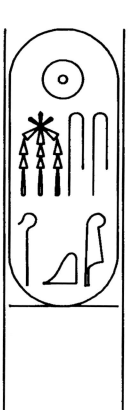

RAMESSES I

◁

The god Osiris followed by Anubis and Horus.

▽

The god Osiris sitting on his throne with Iun-Mutef (literally *Pillar of his Mother*, epithet of the young Horus and a priestly title), offering eternal peace to the deceased king.

▽ ▷

The god Khepri with a scarab's head, symbolizing the rising sun, sitting on his throne.

The god Atum (not visible here) before five of the nine deities who are known as the *masters of provisions.*

A scene from the *Book of the Gates*. Ram-headed Re, holding the sceptre and the *ankh* and standing on the sun-boat, is protected by the serpent Mehen coiled around his shrine. Another serpent, symbol of prosperity, is standing upright. *(full scene on page 39)*

Book of the Gates. The sun-god Re in his shrine, on the solar bark, is protected by the serpent Mehen. At the front of the boat is Sia, god of wisdom, at the rear Heka, god of magic.

▷▷

Horus with the double (white and red) crown of Upper and Lower Egypt.
(page 42, a detail from the picture on page 43)

▷▷

Ramesses I, welcomed by Anubis, god of embalmment, and Horus, son of Isis, wearing the double Egyptian crown. *(page 43)*

▽ and ▷

The so-called bark of the earth, shaped as a pole, carried by eight mummified figures. Eight deities are seated on top of it and at both ends, which are shaped like cow's heads, there stands a bull.

42

△
Detail of the *First Hour of the Book of the Gates.*

SETHOS I

SETHOS II

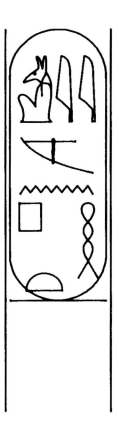

A detail of the king's apron with the two cartouches of Sethos II.

Litany of the sun-god. The crocodile.
(a detail from the full scene on page 49)

◁ ,◁▷ and ▷▷

Litany of the sun-god. The solar disc, with Re and Khepri driving away the evil forces in the shape of various animals fleeing away from both sides of the sun.

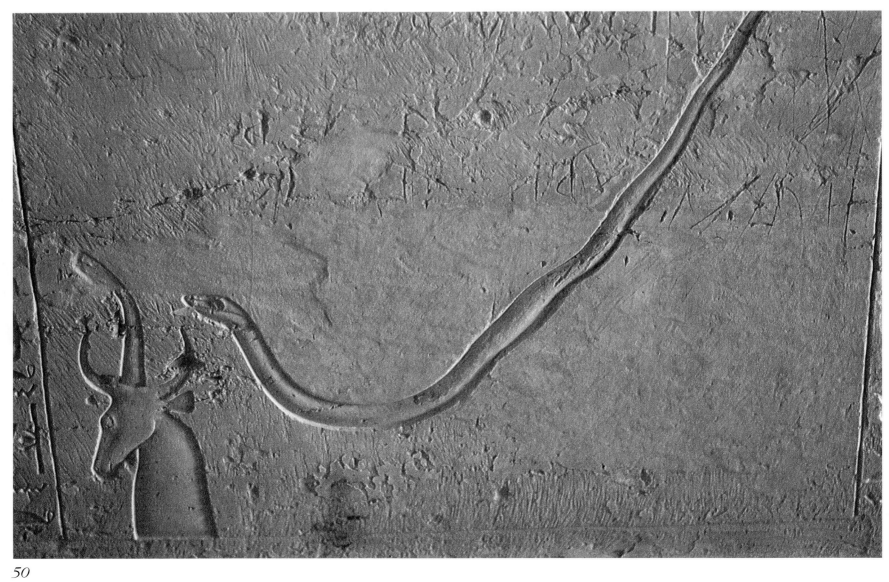

SETHNAKHT

54

The earth god Geb, Nut's husband. *(page 52)*

A pillar representing the god Horus, son of Isis, wearing the double crown. *(page 53)*

▽

Symbolical representation of the *birth of the hours.*

◁

The god Osiris on a throne in his shrine. At the top, the sign of the West is holding two *was* sceptres between two Anubis jackals. Standing on the lotus flower are the four sons of Horus.

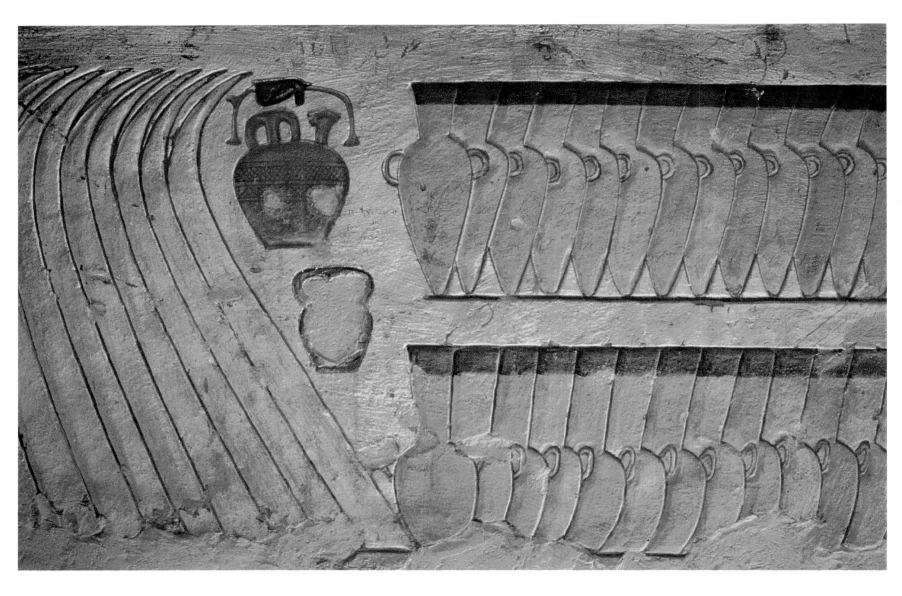

Vases and ivory stored in one of the side-rooms of the tomb.

RAMESSES III

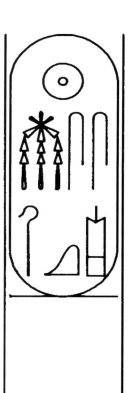

◁▽

Three *uraeus* deities : Renenutet, Hu and Jefa.

▽

Three deities, symbolizing Egyptian towns or provinces, bring offerings to the deceased king.

58

RAMESSES IV

The reed and the bee, hieroglyphic signs meaning king of Upper and Lower Egypt.

Ceiling. The air-god Shu lifting up the sky goddess Nut.

Two hieroglyphics which read *w* and a sound that does not exist in English.

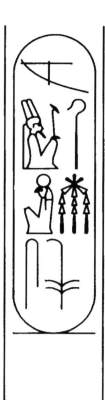

▽

A detail from the ceiling with astronomic figures.

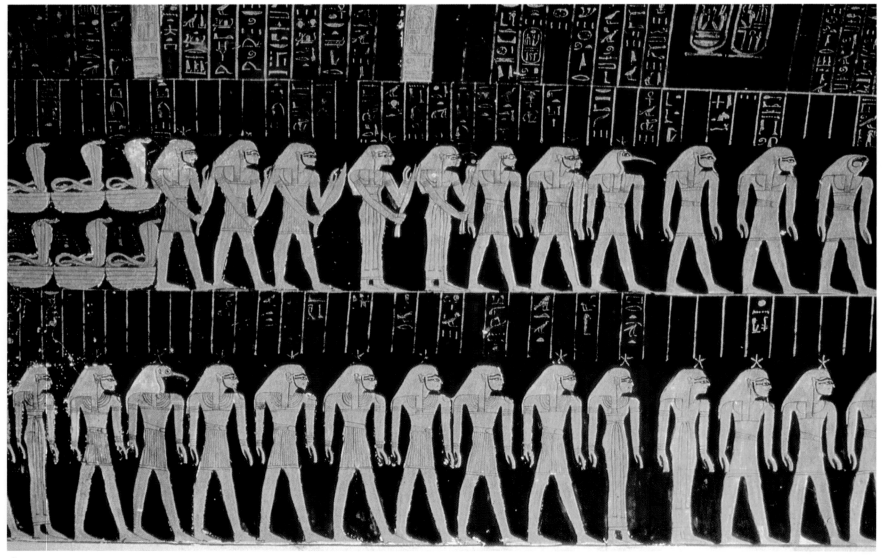

RAMESSES VI

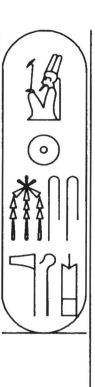

 Ceiling. Book of the day (solar disc) and book of the night (stars). The journey of the sun passes through the body of Nut, the sky goddess. At dawn the sun emerges from her womb; at sunset the solar disc is swallowed by Nut and travels on within her.

▽

The king on the boat of the sun-god between a god and a goddess.

64

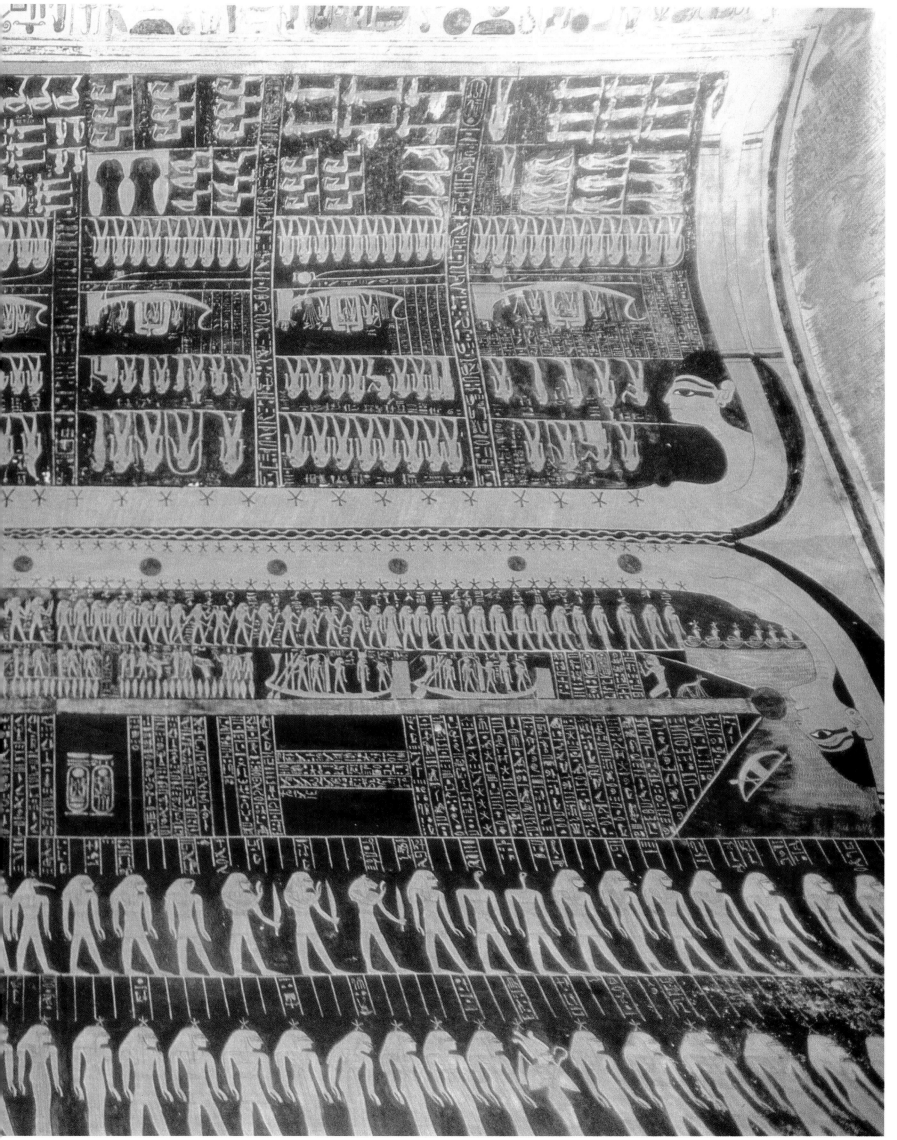

◁

A detail from the ceiling representing constellations.

▷▷

A detail from the ceiling : the sun being swallowed by the sky goddess Nut in the evening, before emerging from her womb again the following morning.

▽

Figures taken from the ceiling with astronomic representations.

◁

A detail showing the king's names hanging down from the winged sun-disc. On both sides *uraei* with the signs of life and prosperity.

▽

A boat bearing the symbol of the goddess Hathor, a woman's head with cow's ears, wearing a *sistrum*. At the front, a scarab meaning "to become", i.e. the sun-god at dawn.

The mummified god Ptah and Maat, goddess of Truth and Justice, wearing an ostrich-feather on her head.

The ram-headed god Re on his boat sailing in the desert.

The morning sun being born in the shape of a scarab and protected on either side by the *ujat* eye, sails on a boat, the stem and stern of which consist of arrow-shooting serpents.

The ram-headed god Re.

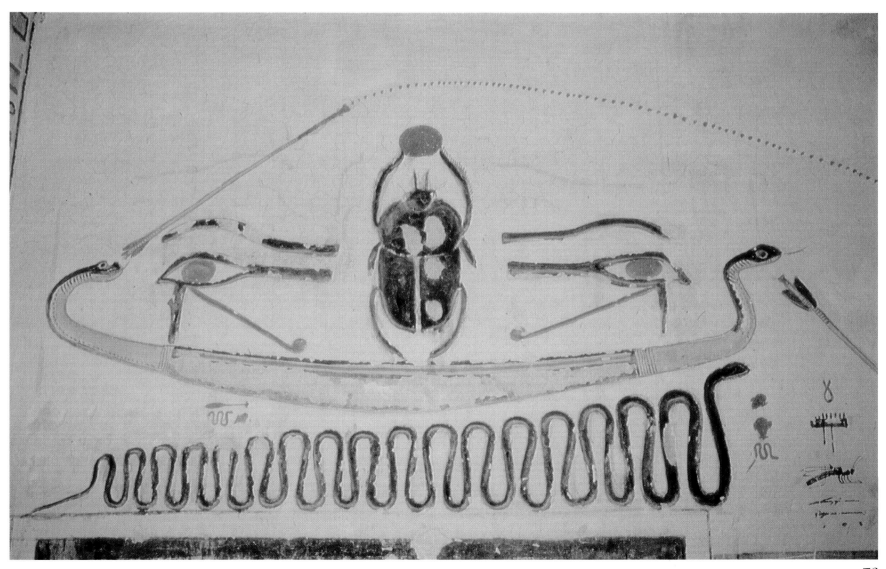

CHAPTER II

SHEIKH ABDEL GURNA

THE NOBLES' TOMBS

REKHMIRE

A huge silver (?) jar is being hammered or polished by two craftsmen. *(page 76, top)*

Egyptians were clever woodworkers. Carpenters are seen manipulating precision instruments. One of them is sawing his stock into planks, whilst others are drilling holes into a lion-shaped bed on the places where the ropes will later be attached. *(page 76, bottom)*

A fragment of a hieroglyphic inscription. *(page 77, top)*

Harps and mandolas were commonly used instruments. A professional harpist and a female mandola-player are providing musical entertainment at a feast in Rekhmire's house. *(page 77, bottom)*

Tomb of Userhet. The enlistment of young army recruits, being shaved by barbers in open air.

USERHET

▽

Food distribution to the troops. Bread in baskets and drinks are placed in front of the squatting soldiers.

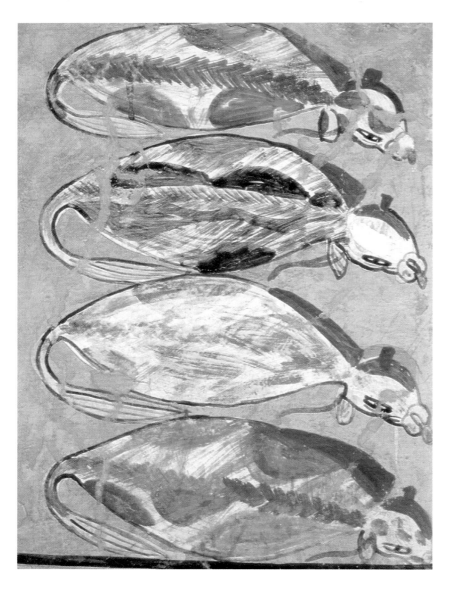

SENNUFER

Offering of four slaughtered oxen. *(left)*

Four bulls pulling Sennufer's funeral boat. *(right)*

◁ ▽

The *sem* or funeral priest, wearing a leopard's skin, is lustrating Sennufer and his wife Merit. *(a detail from the illustration below)*

▽

Sennufer and his wife Merit are lustrated by the *sem* priest wearing a leopard's skin. Sennufer is holding some lotus flowers, whereas Merit holds the sacred *menat* necklace in her right hand and a *sistrum* and a lettuce leaf in her left hand.

Merit offering a cup to her seated husband who is holding a bouquet of flowers.

The pilgrimage to Osiris in Abydos was one of the dearest wishes of all Egyptians during their life-times. Those who couldn't achieve this goal, tried at least to have it represented in a picture. In the upper register a bark is sailing down the Nile, visualized as a white zigzag band, while another one is sailing up-stream with the aid of the North wind in the lower register.

Sennufer and his daughter Mut-tuy are sitting in front of two rows of men who are bringing in offerings : necklaces, leather sandals, a piece of cloth, two *ushabtis*, a mask, a heart-shaped amulet, etc...

Fowling scene in the marshes.

Birds flying over papyrus thickets.

Detail from a banquet scene : chatting ladies.

Dancing girl between two musicians at a banquet.

NAKHT

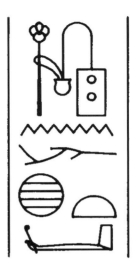

◁

The Western goddess.

▷▷

Tomb of Khaemhet. The god Osiris with the Western goddess.

(full scene page 91, bottom right - details page 90 and 91)

▽

A thirsty sailor drawing water from the Nile.

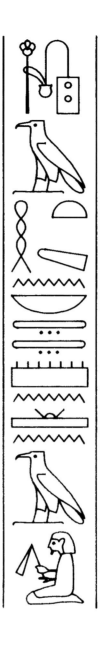

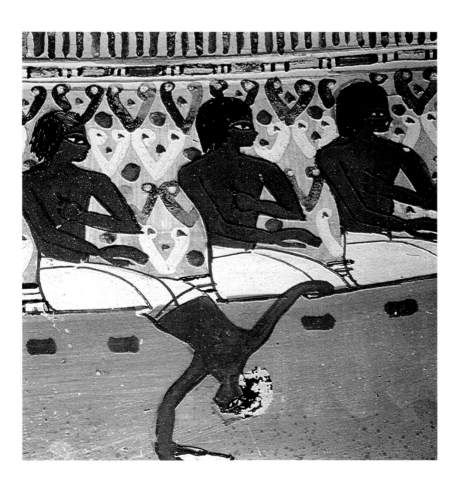

KHAEMHET

◁◁

Three court officials respectfully incline themselves before the Pharaoh.

▽

Khaemhet was overseer of the royal granaries under Pharaoh Amenophis III. His tomb is decorated with beautiful reliefs.

RAMOSE

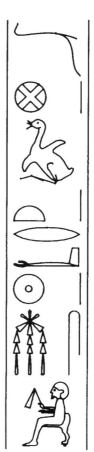

▷▷

A lady called Ipuia, wife of Neby, Ramose's father.

▽

A detail from an offering table. Lotus flowers and onions.

A detail from a hieroglyphic inscription with Ramose's titles and name.

A detail from the funeral procession : the mourners.

Offering of geese (detail).

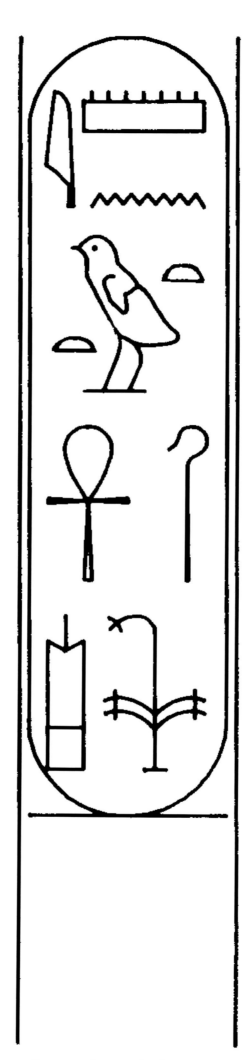

*Cartouche with the name
of king Tutankhamon*

CHAPTER III

DEIR EL MEDINA

THE CRAFTSMEN'S GRAVES

Tomb of Sennejem.   The jackal-headed demon, guardian of the 9th gate of the underworld.

Fishing with a draw-net on the Nile.

SENNEJEM

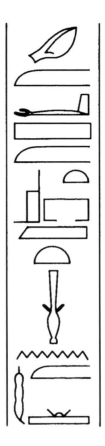

Sennejem and his wife Iyneferti (detail).

The *benu* bird on the bark of Re.

The god Thot and two demons in the under-world.

Demon with a serpent's head, guardian of the 6th gate in the underworld.

Sennejem and his wife Iyneferti adoring gods in the underworld (detail).

Three demons in the underworld.

110

◁

The goddess Isis, represented as a falcon and watching over the mummy.

▽

The god Osiris in his shrine.

◁

The dog-headed demon, guardian of the 10th gate of the underworld.

▷

Sennejem and his wife Iyneferti harvesting and tearing out flax in the fields of Iaru.

▷▷

Offerings to Osiris.

▷▷▷

Sennejem and his wife Iyneferti worshipping the gods of the underworld. *(page 114)*

▽

Sahti, wife of Khabekhnet, himself a son of Sennejem, with a lotus flower and a perfume cone on top of her head.

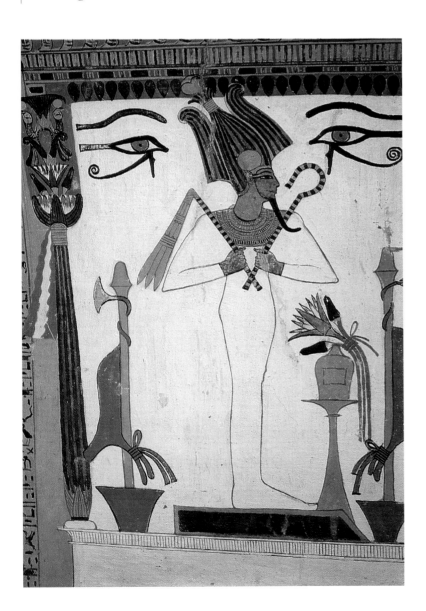

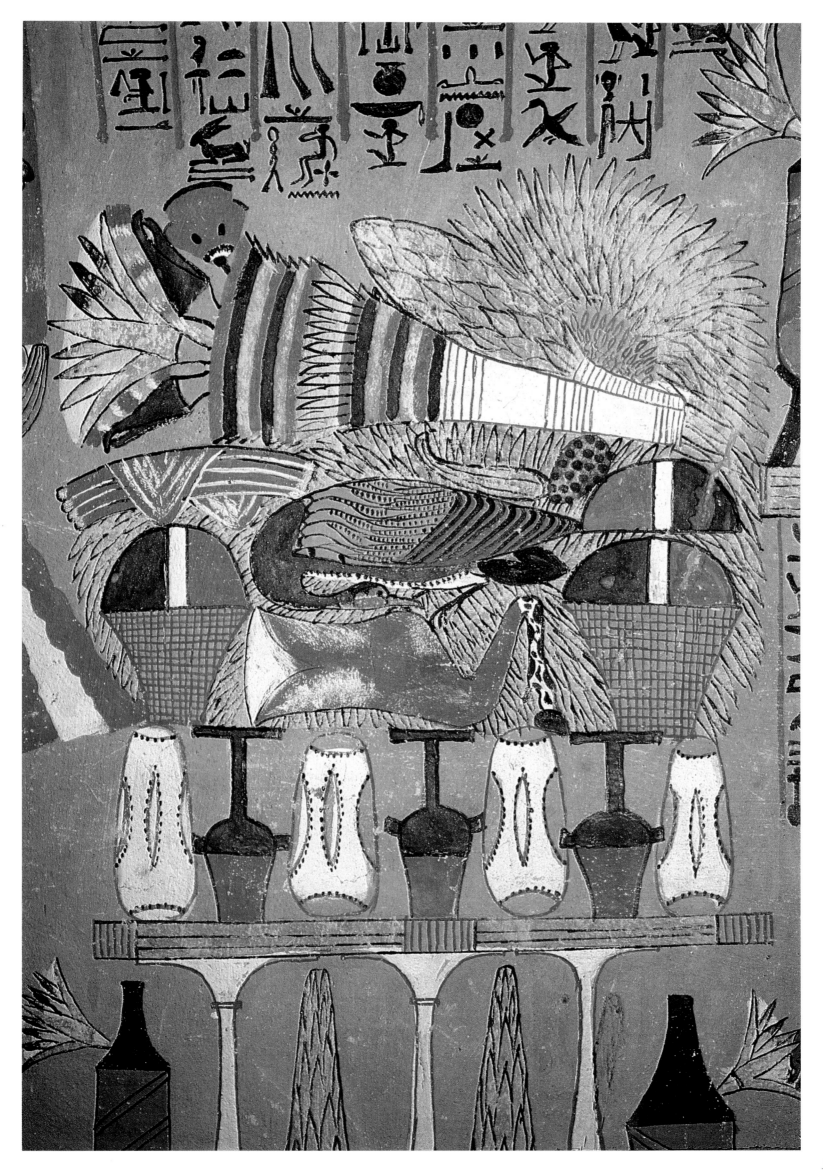

INHERKHA

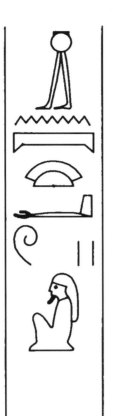

118

A serpent called "son of the earth" in the underworld (a detail from the *Book of the Dead*). *(page 115, top)*

Inherkha adoring the four *sab* jackals, supposed to draw the solar bark in the underworld. *(page 115, bottom)*

Inherkha, with shaven head, facing the three jackal-headed demons, the souls of the West, i.e. the Necropolis.

Inherkha, holding a brazier and wearing a leopard's skin, is offering some geese to Osiris.

The two *aker* lions sitting back to back, supporting the horizon, are called *Yesterday* and *Tomorrow* and they symbolize the idea of eternity.

Relatives offering to the deceased and his wife (who are out of picture!)

A hawk-headed divinity carrying out the ritual of *the opening of the mouth* on the upright mummy.

Inherkha, holding a brazier, is standing before the god Ptah (not in the picture) with his son Harmin.

▽

Inherkha and his wife Waab listening to the harpist's song.

▷

Inherkha facing his *ba* or soul, a bird with a human head.

The solar bark with the goddess Isis in front, followed by Thot with the ibis head, Khepri with the scarab's head, symbol of the rising sun, a deity called *Hu* which means *authoritative utterance* and, finally, Inherkha himself, assuming the role of helmsman.

The scarab *Kheper* with the *menat* necklace,
an attribute of the goddess Hathor.

▷

Inherkha with a brazier adoring Osiris

Tomb of Inherkha. A wild cat, friend of the sun or Re himself, slaying the serpent Apophis, the sun's enemy, coiled around the tree of Heliopolis.

Tomb of Nefertari. The winged goddess Maat at the entrance of the sloping passage leading down to the burial chamber.

CHAPTER IV

BIBAN EL HARIM

THE VALLEY OF THE QUEENS

NEFERTARI

◁

One of the two *aker* lions supporting the sun in his horizon, an image derived from Chapter XVII of the *Book of the Dead*.

◁◁

The god Harmachis and the goddess Hathor, mistress of the West.

▽

Queen Nefertari led before Osiris, god of the underworld, by the goddess Isis.

▽ ▷

Queen Nefertari worshipping the sacred cows.

Queen Nefertari offering cloth to the god Ptah.

△
Iun-mutef or "pillar of his mother", one of the
names of the god Horus.

▷

Queen Nefertari being conducted into the underworld by Horus (out of picture).

▽

The *benu* heron or phoenix, in Chapter XVII of the *Book of the Dead*, considered as a symbol for the sun-god, and the goddess Nephthys, in the form of a falcon.

▽

Guardian of the Fifth gate of the underworld.

The vulture-goddess Nekhbet above the entrance of a side-room in the tomb.

Queen Nefertari offering wine to the goddesses Isis, Nephthys and Maat.

The ram-headed god Re represented as a mummy supported by the goddesses Isis and Nephthys.

144

◁
A monkey with a bow and two baboons, demons of the underworld.

▷▷
Ramesses III worshipping the gods.

◁

▷
The goddess Neith, patron-goddess of Sais, a
city in the delta.

146

KHAEMWESET

◁

Antelope-headed demon, guardian of the 9th gate in the underworld.

◁◁

Ramesses III, his head covered with the *nemes*.

▽

Ramesses III, with the solar disc above him, stands in adoration.

A vulture-headed demon, guardian of the 16th gate in the underworld.

Ramesses III and his son burning incense.

152

153

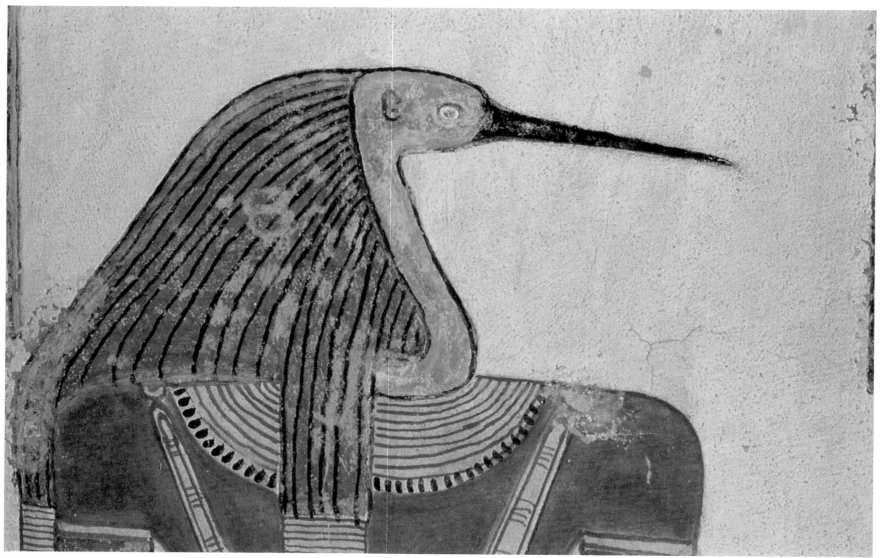

A naked demon called Herimaat at the entrance of the innermost chamber.

Ramesses III with the white crown of Upper Egypt, offering incense to Re.

Demon with a bird's head, guardian of one of the gates in the underworld.

Ramesses III, followed by his son, welcomed
by the air-god Shu.

Hapi, one of the four sons of Horus.

155

◁
Ramesses III in adoration.

◁
Ramesses III in adoration.

A dog-headed deity of the underworld, followed by a youthful Horus with a falcon's
head, also called the *Beneficent Horus.*

The god Shepes with the crescent and the disc of the moon.

The goddess Nephthys before Osiris. Inbetween these two deities, the four sons of Horus on top of a lotus flower.

The ibis-headed god Thot with the moon's crescent and disc.

Ramesses III wearing the blue *khepresh* or so-called war helmet, incensing the god Horus.

◁

The young prince.

▷

One of the guardians of the gates in the underworld, with a jackal's head.

▷▷

Demon with a cat's head, guardian of one of the gates in the underworld.

▽

Pharaoh Ramesses III, adoring the gods.

King Ramesses III welcomed by Re-Harma-chis.

Ramesses III and his son, holding an ostrich-feather fan, are being welcomed by the god Imset, one of the four sons of Horus.

AMEN HER KHOPSHEF

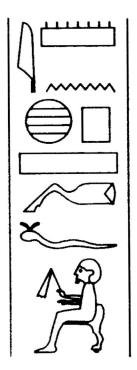

▽

A winged serpent with the *shen* seal.

▷

The god Ptah-Tatenen welcoming king Ramesses III and his son.

170

Ramesses III welcomed by the god
Ptah-Tatenen.

The mummy-like god Ptah in his shrine, holding a sceptre composed of the symbolic
elements *djed* (stability), *ankh* (life) and *was*
(prosperity).

Ramesses III burning incense in front of the
god Ptah.

◁

The royal prince with a side-curled hairlock, symbol of youth.

▽

Sematy, a ram-headed demon, guardian of the 6th gate in the underworld.

The jackal-headed god Duamutef, one of the four sons of Horus, welcoming Ramesses III and his son (detail).

Khutjetef, a demon with a vulture's head, guardian of the 8th gate in the underworld.

(continued from page 16)

pared to the much more elaborate ones of the funeral chapel on the surface which, without doubt, only very few Egyptologists have had the privilege to visit. Alas, these paintings have lost their freshness and require some serious cleaning.

We should recall, however, that at one time in the past, the tomb of Rekhmire (100) had become so dirty that one could hardly, if at all, distinguish the wonderful paintings it contained. The patient restorations, carried out during World-War II by Egyptian specialists, formed by the French expert Alexandre Stoppelaëre, have now rendered the original freshness to the ancient colours, allowing us to admire the aesthetical qualities of the painterly masterpieces with which this remarkable monument is filled. Two other tombs with well-preserved paintings have been invaded by tourists so frequently that the authorities were forced to deny their access to the general public : they are the tombs of two (apparent) contemporaries, Nakht (52), scribe and astronomer to the god Amun, and Menna (69), scribe of the royal fields. Some of the most characteristic examples of the graceful art which characterizes the middle of the XVIIIth Dynasty can be seen here, a period so fascinating that one is tempted to label it the **quattrocento** of Pharaonic history.

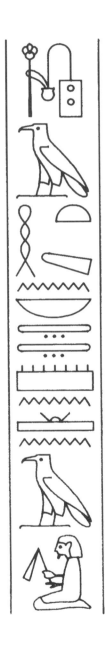

The title and name
of Menna, scribe of the royal fields

CHAPTER III

DEIR EL-MEDINA
The Craftsmen's Graves

T he third area to which we direct our attention is Deir el-Medina, site of the ancient village where the craftsmen of the Theban Necropolis lived in an almost monastic isolation throughout the New Kingdom. Its location, at the heart of Western Thebes and close to the Valley of the Queens, proved a good choice. It consists of a small *wadi*, embedded between two hills and, in Antiquity, surrounded by fortifications which facilitated the surveillance tasks of the local police such as observing the villagers and preventing them from deserting their work. Deir el-Medina, the Arab name for the locality, which signifies *convent of the city*, is due to the fact that the temple of the Ptolemaic period, dedicated principally to the goddess Hathor, had been inhabited by Coptic monks. The latter, by the way, have not failed to "retouch" some of the original figures and inscriptions fairly hard-handedly. To the North of the temple, itself situated at the entrance of the Valley, foundations of several chapels have been discovered. These were dedicated to the goddess Merseger or Mertseger, *she-who-loves-silence*, supposedly inhabiting the mountain overlooking the village and even the Peak of the West which dominates the entire landscape. These chapels reveal quite a lot about the piety of these craftsmen who, in addition to Merseger, also worshipped the memory of Amenophis I and his mother Ahmes-Nefertari, both deified after their death. So intense was the devotion for this royal couple that celebrations in their honour were held once or sometimes several times a year, in the form of processions during which a statue of the sanctified Pharaoh even oracled.

Bernard Bruyère, under the auspices of the *Institut Français d'Archéologie Orientale du Caire*, explored the site for some 30 years. He succeeded in clearing the ancient village in its entirety, and, in doing so, safeguarded one of the very few remaining Pharaonic agglomerations. Along a straight road, the houses seem glued to each other, squeezed between the street and the wall that once encircled the village. In the course of at least three centuries during which they lived in

this place, the inhabitants must have dwelled in the same houses as their predecessors, inheriting profession and properties from father to son. This can be derived from the fact that no successive superposed layers were discovered, as was normally the case in other ancient sites. The houses are small and narrow, with an average depth of 20 (and even 13) m and a width of 4 m, with the largest being established at 27 x 6 m. Their ground-plan is virtually uniform and consists of a number of rooms placed one after the other : the first room with an alcove bedroom, some kind of reception hall with a higher ceiling supported by a pillar, a storage room for victuals or, in other cases, a bedroom, a staircase leading to the roof and, finally, a kitchen ; in the basement there are, furthermore, one or two cellars accessible from the kitchen and the reception hall. Apparently this type of house did not have a second floor. The average height of these buildings varies from 3 to 5 m. Today their outward appearance is quite lack-lustre, but it is not hard to imagine how they once looked, with plastered and painted walls, the proud abode of an artist or craftsman in charge of the excavation and decoration of the tombs of the Pharaohs in the Valley of the Kings. They are called, with a vague term, *Servants in the Place of Truth*, but, in fact, they even had their own chiefs and scribes. In a way, they formed a brotherhood living in isolation, enjoying the privileges of being housed and nourished, but perhaps also experiencing the inevitable inconvenience(s) of promiscuity. Searchers have discovered thousands of *ostraca* in this site, limestone flakes or potsherds used instead of the costly papyrus to write down some of the everyday events which befell them. Studying such a formidable goldmine of information allows for a reconstruction of day-to-day life in Deir el-Medina, the neighbourly quarrels, the domestic disputes, the joys and sorrows of an entire community, insurrections by the craftsmen even, when administrative difficulties occurred or when there were delays in the payment in kind of their wages. The ostraca, for instance, inform us of the names of each of the members of a working-team, of the allocation of tasks, of the tools at their disposal, of the food rations they received. They also shed light on the way justice was done, with the craftsmen creating their proper tribunal to pass judgment, not shunning the occasional "oracle" pronounced by the statue of Amenophis I, patron-saint of the Theban Necropolis. There is the often-quoted and quite unjust case of an unfortunate craftsman named Menna who, during the reign of Ramesses III, had sold some fat to a police-officer. Eleven years on, with Ramesses IV on the throne, the latter had still not settled his debt. The document also informs us that barley had been the proposed means of payment, a common way of bartering at the time. Most striking of all, however, is that the police-officer, who is called Mentmose, puts forward his own brother as guarantor - and supplier of the barley - and his colleagues and the craftsmen as witnesses, in front of whom he condemns himself to 100 strokes with a stick... should he fail to honour his promise! But the impudent officer does go back on his word and poor Menna is left the dupe of the whole affair.

The ostraca provide us with various other pieces of invaluable information. They refer, for example, to the classical authors whose texts the youths studied and copied (incorporating some spelling-mistakes, due to their imperfect command of the ancient language), and also to the most familiar religious hymns and the most popular deities. Beside these writings in cursive characters, the so-called *hieratic writing*, we may also encounter some exercises in hieroglyphics. Here the aspiring artist is caught in the act, revealing his painstaking efforts and unremitting zeal to become an excellent calligrapher. And what to say of the drawings on some of the ostraca? They are quite charming, some are genuine first drafts traced by a master hand, others seemingly copied from a model by apprentices. Then again we might find illustrations to beast-fables, the texts of which, unfortunately, have not come down to us, or even the odd caricature: the profile of an unshaven Pharaoh, rumours of matrimonial squabbles at the palace, taking on the form of a chariot fight between the king and the queen exchanging arrows, the portrait of a comrade (mentioned by name) striking a comical pose, etcetera... The feeling prevails that these people, condemned to lead a hard and isolated life, toiling in the most arid of landscapes, exposed to the scorching heat for most of the time, far from the diversions of Thebes on the right bank of the Nile - at that time, lest we forget, the centre of the civilized world - experienced a great urge to indulge in some sound foolery every so often. And among the scarce means they had at their disposal to do so, their art provided the most satisfying outlet. These humble drawings, so full of zest and liberty, constitute an eloquent testimony to their thirst for emancipation. We should hasten to add, though, that the craftsmen, much to their credit, never exceeded the limits of decency. The images are never, or only very exceptionally, shocking. It would rather seem that the Egyptians, though not lacking any sense of humour, were a reserved and decent people.

One problem bound to have held the attention of Deir el-

Medina's former responsibles must have been the craftsmen's water-supply. Bernard Bruyère excavated an area to the North of the site and beyond the girdle walls, and emptied an immense and very deep pit which had been dug, with near certainty, to attain the water underground. When the excavation works failed to yield the expected result, they were visibly abandoned and the traditional method of carrying the water from the nearest well in the cultivated zone to the villagers on donkey-back - still in use today, by the way - was soon restored. The great well, discovered by Bruyère, had, in fact, been converted into a shoot, providing the researchers with well over 3000 ostraca.

The first installations at Deir el-Medina go back to the beginning of the XVIIIth Dynasty, although we know far more of the site's history during the Ramesside period. Face to face with the dwellings described above, stands a hill, strewn with craftsmen's graves, the resting-places of the *Servants in the Place of Truth* as they called themselves. These tombs differ from those of the Nobles in that, to reach their underground burial chambers, one needs to descend a dangerous, often winding staircase. The difficulties surrounding the interment's preparation - introducing the coffins and funeral furniture into the vaults - spring to mind vividly here. On the surface, a small chapel indicated the tomb's location. It was covered by a pointed pyramid made of mud bricks and surmounted by a pyramidion in limestone. Each of its four sides displayed the engraved portrait of the buried person, in whose honour the monument had been erected. Too frail to resist the tooth of time, every single one of these pyramids has now disappeared. Another clear distinction to be made between the artists of Deir el-Medina and their colleagues at Sheikh abdel-Gurna, appears on a stylistic level. The first indeed adopted the technique of the yellow background colour, applied in a thin layer and with a large brush to the mud wall, which had not been treated with a protective layer of stucco. The use of vivid colours makes the figures stand out from the background and treats the onlooker to a fascinating spectacle. Another, quite contrasting, technique, known as "monochrome" and not unlike straightforward drawing, shows the objects and figures outlined in black. From an aesthetical point of view, the art of the Ramessides, when compared to the wonders of the XVIIIth Dynasty, is unmistakably characterized by a certain relaxation, compensated only and sporadically by a picturesque gesture or a dash of intended or casual humour.

In 1906, the Italian Egyptologist Ernesto Schiaparelli discovered the small funeral chapel of the "architect" Kha (8), but, unfortunately, the paintings are in bad shape. Kha was a contemporary of Amenophis II, Thutmosis IV and Amenophis III (1448-1375 B.C.), whose combined reigns coincided with the zenith of Egyptian art. Of much greater importance was the discovery, on the flank of the hill just opposite the chapel (and not *beneath* it, as expected), of the miraculously preserved burial chamber of the same Kha, full of objects in exactly the same emplacement as on the day of the burial. As a special favour, the Antiquities' Department authorized all these pieces to be transported to the Egyptian Museum of Turin, where they are presently exhibited in a very long hall, which both impresses and moves the visitors : sarcophagi and coffins of Kha and his wife Merit, a beautiful flowered wooden statue of Kha, standing on a chair, ten plastered and painted small wooden boxes, some heavy and still unopened jars, an alabaster perfume jug, a bronze vase stand, three *situlae* in copper, two tripods, two tables, an *ushabti* (or funeral figure) box, a box containing the wife's wig, some sticks, a large papyrus scroll containing the *Book of the Dead*, measuring several metres in length, and numerous other artefacts. Thanks to this exceptional discovery, we may form a fairly realistic idea of the lost contents of Deir el-Medina's fifty-odd tombs and of the kind of furniture with which the villagers set up their houses. Admittedly, and moving though it may be, the quality of decoration of e.g. the painted boxes, to cite but one example, is really rather common. Nevertheless we may observe, with some surprise, that the wood, having been covered with stucco first, is then repainted with a décor imitating the very grain of the wood, a technique still in vogue today, notably on the doors of houses and apartments, after the imitation marble which decorates so many of our walls.

A second tomb which is of the utmost importance to the study of Theban painting, and from which all the scenes have been lifted and applied onto canvas to be reconstructed in the Museum of Turin, is the minuscule chapel of May (338), *scribe of drawings* or draughtsman of Amun. The style of the paintings, which, fortunately, have been well-preserved in parts, is typical of post-Amarnian art, which could be situated in the short reign of Tutankhamun (1358-1350 B.C.) and of which we possess virtually no, if any, other examples. To ignore this jewel, which, though invisible in situ, is still accessible to anyone travelling in Italy, would have been terribly unjust. The subjects treated are : the funeral (transport of the sarcophagus to the tomb), the pilgrimage to Abydos and the presentation of offerings to the demised couple, May and Tamit. In addition, the Museum of Turin also preserves a stela which probably comes from the funeral chapel of May and on which all the members of his family have been represented.

Before passing on to the commonly visited burial chambers, mention must be made of another important tomb, closed, sadly but perhaps justifiably enough, to the general public, that of the sculptor Ipuy (217), contemporary of Ramesses II (1298-1235 B.C.). Like so many other still unpublished rock-tombs which perish before our very eyes, this one, edited, fortunately in 1927, has since lost several of its best scenes. Among them, the vintage scene, the whereabouts of which remains totally obscure, whether in the hands of an anonymous collector or, possibly, destroyed. The iconographical wealth of Ipuy's tomb makes it a veritable source of information for our knowledge of everyday life. One entire wall is made up of scenes inspired by the workshops, where

catafalques, statues and ritual objects were being produced. Scores of little details enable us to establish touch with this society of humble people to whom we owe the pure masterpieces of Egyptian art. Ipuy took care not to omit a single essential element, to a degree that we do not only witness the craftsmen's activities, but that we actually become involved in the way these people were treated on a human level. A civilization, so utterly refined and organized as Pharaonic Egypt, could not remain indifferent to the well-being of those who were its modest, but precious artisans. Significant in this respect is the suggestion of working-accidents in Ipuy's tomb : a heavy mallet falls onto the foot of one of the craftsmen, who cries out with pain; an oculist relieves the pain of another worker, clinging convulsively to the shrine he was working on, by administering some eye-lotion. Above this large piece of furniture, the movements of two men, one recumbent, the other holding the first's arm, have inspired quite different interpretations : for some, the scene vividly illustrates the setting of a dislocated shoulder, whilst others maintain the theory of the foreman having to "pull" one of his workers from a deep sleep. Here are three more details from one of the other, completely ruined, walls. First of all, a pastoral scene, a rare, perhaps even unique example in Egyptian iconography. A shepherd is playing the flute and grazing his goats, his bundle hanging from a peculiar stick, which he holds on his shoulder. All in all a rather unpretentious (and fragmentary) scene, which nonetheless sparks off poetical feeling by virtue of its very subject and by the hints of red, blue and green colour which the vases of the scene above, impart to it. There is, secondly, a fishing scene on the Nile, which bursts with energy. Posted on the river banks the men are hauling in their large nets which are crammed with fish. Once the fish taken out, they are piled up into the baskets and brought to the market. An astute kid spies on the fish that are trying to slip through the meshes of the net and catches them in their flight. At one extremity of the picture two workers are quarreling ostentatiously. One is a Southern type with black, woolly hair, a turned-up nose and Negroid mouth. He is visibly nervous and probably hurling abuse at his colleague, who not only has the physical features - aquiline nose and bleached hair - but also the placid character common to Northerners. A scene full of humour, a caricature, so to say, divided into two red masses, outlined in black and standing out against the mud wall, brushed over with yellow paint. In the lower register, a blue strip streaked with black zigzag lines represents the river; in the river fishermen with a net are manoeuvring their small wooden boats amidst the lotus flowers. Contrast, this time, is evoked by the clash of red and azure. Three seated men are paddling to a regular rhythm, indicated by a fourth, upright and fair-skinned character, who is shouting out commands. Every trait has been simplified to the extremest, but nevertheless expresses the animation perfectly. A curious detail which recurs in these concise drawings of the Ramesside period, is that the neck's juncture is marked by a curved line, which one would suppose to be the collar of a tunic, but the torso is uncovered! (p. 104).

The majority of Deir el-Medina's other tombs are, as we have stated before, underground burial chambers, vaulted rooms with representations relating to the next world. The best-preserved and most richly coloured of these burial chambers is that of Sennejem (1) *Servant in the Place of Truth*, who belonged, apparently, to the XIXth Dynasty. Every wall without exception has been covered with scenes that almost reach the floor, scenes in which the deceased and his wife Iyneferti appear in front of a long series of gods, goddesses and demons of the underworld. No sooner has the visitor stepped into this tomb, than he is struck by the symbolism of its images, which, in themselves, lack aesthetical value. Re is there, springing forth at dawn from the Eastern mountain, whence he is born; this notion is given concrete form to by the image of a woman's arms and breasts holding the solar disc above a small desert valley. Having reached the zenith, the sun settles down again in his double horizon, upheld by two lions. Then he has to make ready for his nocturnal course, which will be strewn with obstacles he has to overcome. This thought is materialized by the image of a cat, cutting off a serpent's head with its knife. Inside the tomb, on the vault, Re is shown travelling in his bark, whilst Sennejem, in the process of opening the door which separates heaven from earth, also penetrates into the underworld. There he will worship the deities who welcome him into their company. The goddess of the sky, all motherly, emerges as a sycamore fairy with human appearance and offers bread and water to the deceased and his wife, who have come up to her by breaking through the roof of their tomb. Its four decorated walls, on the other hand, revive the myth of Osiris with the green complexion, all wrapped up in mummy swathes, leaving only his hands free, so that he can cross the emblems of royalty over his shoulders (p. 111, bottom left). The tiara from which the solar disc emerges, covers his head. Standing upright underneath an ornamental canopy which, by its uraeus, its multi-coloured cornice and its little floral columns, recalls that of the Pharaohs, the god of the dead, painted on a white background and firmly in contrast with the rest of the burial chamber which is painted yellow, is the first scene which catches the eye of the visitor. The strident colours of the offerings heaped up in front of him indeed make his presence all too conspicuous. A little bit further on, Anubis, here assuming the role of guide of the underworld, proceeds with the embalmment of Osiris' body. Just opposite, the mummy is watched over by Isis and Nephthys, both metamorphosed into falcons. The Eastern wall is the most famous : it is entirely dedicated to the Fields of Ialu (Iaru in old Egyptian), high above which the sun god, in his bark, is being worshipped by blue baboons. The Egyptian paradise floats on the ocean. Charming flowers grow on it, as well as fruit-trees : sycamores, date and *dum* palms. The deceased couple, in order to merit to live there, have to carry out the agricultural tasks vital to the prosperity of the divine domain. So they set about ploughing the land, sowing the grain, extracting the flax, reaping the corn, gathering the ears...(p. 112) Once the work accomplished, Sennejem and his wife set foot on the island of the blessed and kneel down in adoration before the Masters of the Universe : Re, Osiris and Ptah. Behind these deities, a young man paddling a papyrus boat, turns around to take a look at the newcomers. He is one of the deceased's sons, who probably died at a very young age and entered into bliss before his parents. The sheer ingenuousness with which the whole is represented and the exceptional state of preservation makes us turn a blind eye at the mediocrity of style for a moment. Reduced space forced the artist to flatten his figures. The dryness of the strokes, the lack of vigour in the lines - especially in the agricultural scenes - is compensated only by a strong composition : a large yellow rectangle framed by blue strips (the celestial Nile and its stylized waves) with the different scenes placed inbetween one above the other; a field of red corn, one rich with green flax, an orchard with trees alternately coloured green or brown striped with black, and, finally, the flowered garden with its fan-shaped bushes painted green, blue and red. The south wall's inferior register, on either side of the entrance constitutes a genuine family album. All the brothers and sisters and even other blood relatives have been portrayed there. As space ran out, they were squeezed together and, if necessary, emaciated. A closer, isolated look at Sennejem's daughter, upright beneath her mother's chair, will give a fair sample of the decay of Egyptian painting at the end of the Ramesside period. The wall is coarse, the drawing careless, the colours crude and even the child's ludicrous profile might well have been unintended. The objection might then be raised that this particular tomb belonged to a rather humble person, an artisan, a workman even who, at the time, would probably have ranked amongst the lower social classes. Suffice it to say that the sumptuous tombs of the sons of Ramesses III, situated in the Valley of the Queens (Chapter IV), suffered the same fate. There, self-evidently, the wall-decorations are extremely well-executed, to the extent of becoming over-wrought, but what coldness of style in revenge! One can really feel how the Egyptian artist has lost the inspiration that once animated him.

With the above description of Sennejem's burial chamber, written in a poetical, rather than a scientific vein, we have only contemplated to render the scenes, drawn from the *Book of the Dead* - where the vignettes, on papyrus, are arranged in a seemingly arbitrary succession - more logical and intelligible for the Cartesian mind. It was this book, indeed, which inspired the people of Deir el-Medina to decorate the walls of their tombs. To the experts, comparisons and variants still remain very instructive, no matter how tiring certain unavoidable repetitions might become eventually. To quote but one, we might casually refer to the curious example of Sennejem's son, Khabekhnet (2), also bearer of the title *Servant in the Place of Truth*, whose tomb practically abuts on his father's. It shows us the recumbent mummy of Osiris taking on the form of a large fish, guarded by the tiny-looking deities Isis and Nephthys, kneeling above the symbolic plants of North and South, papyrus and lily respectively. At both ends of the bed four black, mummy-like figurines represent the four sons of Horus - Imset, Hapi, Duamutef and Kebehsenuf - guardians of the deceased's entrails. Anubis, with the jackal's head, is wrapping up the body of a *lates*, a fish worshipped in Latopolis (present-day Esna), and represented here for no apparent reason.

Next to the tomb of Sennejem lies the tomb of Inherkha (359), equally well-frequented by tourists and related to a second tomb (299) in its vicinity. Here we have a person who is far more important, considering that he bears the title of Foreman in the Place of Truth. Judging from the style of paintings, he should be situated at a later date, approximately the middle of the XXth Dynasty or the reigns of Ramesses III and Ramesses IV (12th century B.C.). He ordered the excavation of two burial chambers right underneath his principal tomb (359), accessible by two staircases. In the first - vaulted - chamber, decorations have been badly preserved and, to make matters worse, some fragments have undeniably been removed since Lepsius visited the tomb in the middle of the last century. It is thanks to this German scholar's drawings that we may assess some of the damage that has been caused. Either the deceased and his wife Waab are - or rather were - worshipping several deities of the underworld, or they are being brought offerings to. Under a canopy, they play the game called *senet,* a word often translated by draughts. An infrequent scene represents Inherkha seated alone on a papyrus canoe, arms open, stretching a large white scarf, which hints at the pilgrimage to Abydos. A painting of chief interest here - though now deteriorated and partly destroyed - shows the upright figure of the deceased, followed by his wife, incensing a succession of 20 kings and queens enthroned in two rows. The assumption that these are formerly deified sovereigns, might be right. The scene is all the more interesting for the representation - now lost - of a painter holding his palette and squatting at one end of the picture. It is eminently obvious that it is Hui, the artist who decorated this tomb, appending his signature to his work in this highly original manner. The second chamber, vaulted as well, is virtually intact - with the exception of a few details - and stuns the visitor by the sheer perfection of its preservation. The scenes on the wall resemble - although not in style - the ones of Sennejem (1): they are illustrations of the *Book of the Dead,* distributed between the North and South walls and divided into three registers, totalling about 30 vignettes. Among the most important scenes are the deceased face to face with his soul - a bird with human head - standing upright above the tomb p. 124-125); the deceased worshipping a statue of Ptah, the god of Memphis; a swallow perched on a miniature mountain, image drawn from the chapter on the possible metamorphoses of the deceased; the sun on its horizon, supported by two *aker* lions sitting back to back, and whose very names, Yesterday and Tomorrow, sum up the concept of Eternity (p. 120-121); the worshipping of a large Guardian Serpent, called *Son of the Earth* (p. 115, top); the four black *Sab* jackals, who have to draw the sun-bark on which Inherkha wishes to mount in order to achieve immortality (p.

115, bottom); a god with a falcon's head carrying out the rite of *the opening of the mouth* on the upright mummy (p. 122, top); Inherkha seated before a standard bearing the *ka* sign and then, on a large scale, the hieroglyph of the West, place of the blissful souls; just opposite these scenes, Inherkha, resuscitated from his tomb, illuminated by the rays of the sun (an image which should, logically, have concluded all the other vicissitudes); the deceased couple - two seated white mummies - navigating to heaven in a papyrus bark, driven by their son and, underneath, a great black scarab, the *kheper* or symbol of "coming into being", holding a large necklace - also symbolical - called *menat* (p. 127); the god Thot with the ibis-head introducing our man to Osiris, who is here assuming the role of judge of the dead and to whom Inherkha recites his *declaration of innocence*, in other words, a list of sins which he never committed; a navigation scene, yet again, though this time the four passengers are none less than the deities Isis, Thot, Kheper and Hu, with Inherkha at the helm (p. 126); undoubtedly a representation of four regions of the underworld; the deceased kneeling before a gigantic lotus flower, rising from the water, alluding, perhaps, to the myth of the sun originating from the primary ocean; Inherkha kneeling in adoration before three jackal-headed demons, also on their knees, left arms raised in the air, representing the souls of the West, alias the Necropolis (p. 116-117); the deceased standing before a magnificent blue phoenix, wearing a white crown with two ostrich-feathers (the common head-gear of Osiris), which the texts call *benu* or soul of Re, with the power to authorize his worshipper to leave and enter as he pleases; Anubis with a jackal's head returning to the mummy its heart, a gesture of resurrection; Inherkha, badly shaven in token of mourning, kneeling and worshipping a great falcon; a wild cat, ally of the sun, slaying, with a knife, the serpent Apophis, enemy of Re, under the *ished* tree of Heliopolis, a scene unrolling itself before the eyes of one Nakht-em-Mut, father of Khonsu, both successors to Inherkha as foremen (p. 130); and, finally, above the latter, the drawing of an empty net, signifying, it would seem, that the resident of the tomb has avoided all the pitfalls on his journey successfully.

This long enumeration reveals the iconographic wealth of Inherkha's second tomb. In reality, these paintings occupy only the two superior registers, whereas the third register, almost touching the ground, is mainly reserved to scenes representing offerings to the dead. On the South wall Inherkha and his wife Waab are shown seated and holding each other no less than three times, while they are being incensed and aspersed with cleansing water by two of their sons on the one hand and by six men with shaved heads on the other (p. 119). The man in front, wearing a leopard's skin, is a *sem*, a funeral priest. Four of them are sons of Inherkha, the two remaining men are brothers. The third scene shows a harpist with the upper part of his fatty body bared, kneeling down on a plaited mat and singing, with a grimace, the famous "epicurean" chant, the lyrics to which are reproduced in their entirety on the wall behind him (p. 123). Here are some extracts, which have been derived from Siegfried Schott's translation :

"Thou hast built a house in the sacred land. May thy name live on there. Thy work in the Necropolis is magnificent, thy position in the West excellent... Have a happy day, Inherkha, let not thy heart become weary, have a very nice celebration with the woman thou cherishest in thy heart. Don't torment thy heart for as long as thou livest... Let the people sing before thee, do not recall the evil things which the god also detests. Think of happiness, o man... Inebriate thy heart every day, until the day thou hast to disembark..."

(to which could be added implicitly *"...on the land that loveth the silence"*, as is the case in other versions of the same poem).

On the North side, also near the bottom, we see, first of all, the couple seated before a table of offerings, flanked by a scene in which Inherkha, seated and on his own, receives homages - if that is the right way to term it - from a funeral priest or *sem*, who is holding a censer and the typical instrument required for the ceremony of *the opening of the mouth*, followed by eight men and two women; lastly a scene which, if it were not for the context, could easily pass as a family portrait. For a fleeting moment one would indeed believe to be the guest in an ancient living-room. Inherkha and his wife, both richly dressed in ample white robes, are seated before an ornamental table on which a tart with sycamore-figs has been equilibrated. Four persons - three men and a woman - are carrying objects of a ritual nature rather than gifts : a small box containing *ushabtis* or funeral figures, a statuette of Osiris, god of the dead, libation vases, a censer, a perfume jar containing, without any doubt, sacred oil. The religious contents of the image is undeniable. The artist has, nevertheless, attempted to apply a human, even a humorous touch to it all. The elderly couple is surrounded by its four, naked grandchildren, three little girls, the first of whom is sitting right on top of her grandfather's feet, and a tiny boy. These four children have "baroque" hairdressings: locks of hair, some straight, some curly, separated from each other by a shaved area. In addition, the girls wear earrings and necklaces. They are all holding a little bird in their hand or perhaps they are passing it around. Excluded from this game, their younger brother turns away, throws his arms into the air and hits his grandmother's knees with both hands. The inscription next to him describes the boy as irascible; it merely states : *"son of his son, Inherkha* (the same name as the grandfather), *nicknamed the Violent"*. This picturesque detail comes quite unexpected in an otherwise sinister burial chamber, where, after all, everything but the harpist's song, recalls the idea of Death and Hell. But it is somehow typical of ancient Egyptians that, although we consider imperturbable gravity to be one of their main traits of character, they, in fact, never lose their sense of humour. Closer study of the works of the painters of the New Kingdom, and more particularly of those of the Ramesside period, trained at Deir el-Medina, reveals that these realistic little scenes, now moving, then again amusing, were often introduced into their compositions.

As for the style of Inherkha's tomb, it is quite different from that of Sennejem. If anything, it is generally more polished. The strokes have been applied more vigorously, the colours do not clash nearly as blatantly. The yellow background-colour, for one, is far less vivid than with Sennejem. Still we are sometimes taken aback by the immensity of the eyes and by some of the persons' profiles resembling a mouse snout, rather than anything else. It would appear from detailed examination that several painters of varying degrees of skill participated in the execution of this work. If, on the whole, the quality seems superior to that of other works on the site, despite the fairly advanced stage of decadence in Ramesside art, this should be ascribed to the fact that we are dealing with the tomb of a "prominent" figure, not a common hand-worker's.

The name and title of Inherkha, Foreman in the Place of Truth

CHAPTER IV

BIBAN EL-HARIM
Valley of the Queens

In Arabic the Valley of the Queens is called Biban el-Harim, which stands for *Tombs,* literally, *"Doors" of the Ladies.* The expression is well-picked, because it is through these doors that we may enter into the world of the underworld. It has probably not passed unnoticed - especially after the reading of the two preceding chapters - that the common mortal of Ancient Egypt is always, both in life and in death, accompanied by his beloved wife. This, however, is not the case for the Pharaoh. There is not one official monument which represents him with the queen. The one exception to the rule stems from the reign of the revolutionary Amenophis IV - Akhenaten (1375-1358 B.C.) who has always been depicted with the beautiful Nefertiti by his side. In the rock-tombs of the Valley of the Kings, the deceased sovereign, on his nocturnal course, traverses the different stages of hell all by himself, in pursuit of the sun-bark. The supreme god Re also travels without a female companion, whereas other deities are often represented in pairs or even triads : Amun-Mut-Khonsu, Osiris-Isis-Horus, Ptah-Sekhmet-Nefertum, etc... Death, in other words, separates the royal couple. Man and wife are buried as far away from each other as possible, at either extremity of the Theban Necropolis, although still within the same mountain range, dominated by the Peak of the West. from there onwards, they both have to make their own way into the *Amduat,* the Egyptian Hades, as well. Another curious matter is the absence of a hieroglyphic expression corresponding to *queen* : the term used instead reads *royal wife* or *great royal wife,* taking into account that the Pharaohs were polygamists. There exists no exact count of the legitimate wives and concubines of Ramesses II, for instance. Barring miscalculation, no less than a hundred sons and half as many girls have been numbered among his offspring! His exceptionally long (1298-1235 B.C.) and relatively peaceful reign certainly enabled him to enjoy life and to have a great number of spectacular monuments constructed. However, his existence was not exempt from physical suffering altogether, as his mummy reveals the body of an old man immobilized by rheumatism.

Nefertari was Ramesses II's favourite, unquestionably, with a temple of her own in the rocks of Abu Simbel, next to the gigantic rock-temple of her husband, and the most beautiful tomb in the Valley of the Queens, truly one of Egypt's marvels. Unfortunately the artists, instead of sculpturing directly onto the limestone, have applied a more or less thick layer of plaster to the wall, which they have then engraved and painted. With humidity getting free play to affect this ever disintegrating surface, it would soon have turned to dust, had it not been for the rescue operations of the Italian restorers, who have been called in just in time. The first chamber is taken up by the texts and vignettes from the 17th Chapter of the *Book of the Dead.* Amongst the most attractive images, there is a blue heron (the Phoenix), 70 cm in height, whose majestic manner is accentuated by his ethereal colour against the white of the wall, marking it off from the other figures, coloured in various shades of red (p. 138, right): lions between heaven and earth, falcons representing Isis and Nephthys guarding the sarcophagus of Osiris, etc... A painting next to the door, charming by its subject and richly coloured, shows the queen seated in a small edifice, her feet resting on a rush-mat, playing what looks like chess, on her own. The game itself is actually called *senet* by the Egyptians and the recovered rule recalls both the game of draughts and the game of goose. Apparently, spending one's eternal leisure time to this sort of futility, was considered the supreme bliss. Nowadays, would an idle lady be dreaming of playing patience in heaven? For Nefertari, the canopy was gilded - in reality painted yellow - and the entire scene has been varnished as if to preserve it for a longer time than the rest of the tomb's representations. This gloss makes the image stand out and enhances the warmth of the colours : the skin of the queen turns a reddish ochre and the entire painting, framed in green, filled with differently tinted hieroglyphics and patterned with black lines, takes on an exceptional splendour. As for the iconography of the second hall, including, in fact, the descending corridor and the actual burial chamber, it is generally related to the concept of a journey into the underworld. The great queen, mistress of

Egypt and the world, as the inscriptions everywhere report, is taken into the underworld, guided by the gods themselves. At every stage she encounters deities, now infernal, then celestial, seated on their thrones or upright in their shrine. Although she presents every single one of them with a greeting or an offering, she never loses anything of her dignity : sovereign on earth, her beauty eclipses that of the celestial masters who welcome her as a sister, an equal. The tomb's ceiling is sprinkled with yellow stars on a once blue background. It does indeed represent the concept of an ascension into a nocturnal sky. But when, in the end, the queen steps into the depths of the mountain that will protect her, Maat, the goddess of Truth and Justice, daughter of Re, is waiting on the slope with spreaded wings to receive the queen into her arms (p. 131). Justified by this action, Nefertari now passes into Eternity. She does so with all the luxuries of her mortal life : gold, silver and enameled jewellery - diadem, necklace, earrings - forming a perfect frame for her beautiful face; ample, pleated garments in transparent linen embracing her slender body; long, red belts girding her delicate waist elegantly; black kohl to make her almond eyes look longer and liven up the skin of her modelled cheeks. Truly the features, demeanour and gestures of aristocracy!

There are over 70 tombs in the Valley of the Queens, the majority of which are destroyed and uninteresting. A second queen's tomb which deserves to be looked at more closely is that of Thiti, likely wife of an unspecified Ramesses. A long corridor gives into a large hall and three small, side rooms. They show the usual scenes - generally badly preserved - of the various deities to which the queen, whose portrait has been mutilated practically everywhere, presents herself. In the annex to the right of the corridor, there is a painting showing the fairly common subject of the cow Hathor coming out of the Western mountain. The goddess also appears, emerging from the sacred tree, the sycamore, to quench Thiti's thirst.

Other rock-tombs which the tourists never fail to visit are those of sons of Ramesses III, who died prematurely. In this case the Arabic name *harim* is justified, because that is traditionally the place in the palace where the women and children resided together. Ramesses III (1198-1166 B.C.) is the most powerful king of the XXth Dynasty, in fact the last of the great Theban Pharaohs. We are quite well-informed of his reign by some precious documents (papyrus rolls) and texts and bas-reliefs engraved on the walls of the temples which he had constructed at Karnak and especially at Mediner Habu, not far from the Valley of the Queens. From the moment of his accession to the throne, Ramesses III had to reorganize the country's administration after a brief period of troubles and anarchy at the end of the preceding dynasty. He fought some victorious battles, by land and by sea, against enemies seeking to invade the Delta from the North, coming partly from Syria, partly from Libya. The pyramids of hands and phalluses - cut off the corpses of his victims and heaped up in front of him - bear witness to his triumph. Triumphant though he might have been on the battle-field, he was forced to meet the demands of an insatiable clergy, which had become a state within the state, conceding numerous privileges, bestowing them with immeasurable riches, which eventually and inevitably siphoned off the contents of the royal treasury to one single caste. Despite all his efforts, Ramesses III led an unhappy life. Having narrowly escaped a conspiracy staged by one of his viziers at Athribis, one of the Delta cities, he suffered a second, more serious and perhaps even fatal undermining of his royal power, an event which darkened the final years of his life and which, if it did not directly provoke his death, certainly accelerated it. The account of this genuine harem conspiracy can be reconstructed with the help of some miraculously preserved judicial documents. To cut a long story short, one of the wives of Ramesses III, named Tiyi, eager to see her own son placed on the throne, undoubtedly instead of the heir apparent, wants to see the old king eliminated, and she succeeds in persuading several court officials to join the conspiracy. But the plot is revealed and the conspirators, arrested then and there, are led before a court of justice constituted, though not presided, by the king personally. In proportion to their degree of involvement, the accused are either condemned to death or to having their nose and ears cut off. Those condemned to death are left alone in the court-room so that they can carry out the sentence by their own hands. One of the mutilated wretches is so desperate that he also resorts to suicide. There is no mention of the fate of the ambitious and treacherous queen Tiyi, but her son - a mere pawn at the hands of his mother - is executed. The fact whether judgment was passed during the king's own lifetime or, to the contrary, as it is assumed now, under the short reign of his successor and son Ramesses IV, remains another elusive detail. Those who have examined the mummy of Ramesses III closely, derive proof for his sadness from the bitterness of his facial expression. Destiny indeed did not spare him, reclaiming at least four of his sons at a very early age. It is to their memory that he ordered the excavation of sumptuous rock-tombs in the Valley of the Queens.

The word "sumptuous" should be interpreted in the spirit of the Ramesside period (12th century B.C.), a period of affluence, in which dazzling clap-trap was certainly not shunned. Kings and princes, for example, are dressed in outrageously luxurious garments. The artists reverberate this opulence, multiplying the details on the sovereigns' braces, girdles and aprons in the process. The very vividness of the colours they use, bespeaks their desire to show off. But all this is nullified by the sheer lack of inspiration, the manifest conformism, the monotony of these endless processions of trite, academic figures! Alas, this is precisely what fascinates the tourists most, and astonishment at the preservation of these 3000 year old paintings overrides any observation of how aesthetically mediocre and stylistically barren they really are. If these images seem to be getting a greater part in this book than should be coming to them, then the sole reason for this is that they illustrate the "passage to Eternity" very well. They bring us face to face with a multitude of deities, all capable of opening up the way for us, as they had been sensed to do when Ramesses III addressed them in favour of the little boys who had left him so prematurely. The two principal tombs are those of the princes Khaemweset and Amenkhopshef (Amenherkhopshef being his more complete name). Both have been conceived in a similar vein: two long corridors, giving into the burial chamber, with two small side rooms in one or both of the corridors. On the walls, an impressive listing of gods and goddesses represented according to a logic which is beyond us. Depicted among others are: Harmachis, Atum, Geb, Shu, Ptah and Ptah-Sokar-Osiris, Thot, Osiris, Isis, Nephthys, Horus, Anubis, Hathor, the four sons of Horus - Imset, Hapi, Duamutef and Kebehsenuf - Neith, Selqit, not making mention of the demons and the guardians of the gates to the underworld. The only god who is not mentioned is the Theban deity Amun, for the simple reason that he has nothing to do with the underworld. Several gods are easily identifiable by their appearance or attributes, others only by the hieroglyphic inscriptions which the scribe - as a precautionary measure - added to the image and without which every Egyptologist is liable to commit errors of identification.

The name of the
royal prince Khaemweset

CONCLUSION

t the end of these pages describing the four major sectors of the Theban Necropolis, it seems warranted to briefly touch upon the Egyptian philosophy of death again. The actual concept is simple and full of imagery, perhaps even naive. In fact it is the method which the ancient Egyptians adopt to explain this concept, that seems complicated to us. The sun rises in the East and sets in the West. Similarly, the Theban individual conducts his life in the city on the right bank of the Nile, and, after his death, penetrates, like the god Re, into the darkness of the Peak of the West. In doing so he enters into the *land of millions of years* , full of obstacles which he has to overcome, and he traverses the gate or the gates of the underworld leading him to the celestial fields, called Iaru, where he encounters the gods who will purge him of sin. Then he is judged and justified by Osiris, with whom he assimilates himself. *Osiris so and so* means *the late so and so*. At the end of his journey, he reaches Re, Master of the Universe, the uncreated and immortal god, with whom he is unified, so that, every morning at dawn, he may metamorphose as he pleases, becoming, in a word, a "living soul". *Conditio sine qua non* for this is that his mortal remains do not perish so that they can be recognized by the soul, when visiting the tomb, and eventually be reanimated and regenerated. Hence the extreme importance attached to a careful mummification and the need for a vade-mecum to the other world to take along in one's tomb : the so-called *Book of the Dead* for the ordinary citizens and several infernal books for the sovereigns, which have all been copied onto papyrus rolls and reproduced to satiation on the walls of the rock-tombs.

Arpag MEKHITARIAN

BIBLIOGRAPHY

BARGUET, Paul, *Le Livre des Morts des anciens Egyptiens*. Paris, Editions du Cerf, 1967.

BARGUET, Paul, *Les Textes des sarcophages égyptiens du Moyen Empire*. Paris, Editions du Cerf, 1986.

BEINLICH-SEEBER, Christine, und Abdel Ghaffar SHEDID, *Das Grab des Userhat (TT 56)* = Deutsches Archäologisches Institut Kairo, Archäologische Veröffentlichungen 50. Mainz am Rhein, Philipp von Zabern, 1987.

BIERBRIER, Morris, *The Tomb-Builders of the Pharaohs*. London, British Museum, 1982.

BONNET, Hans, *Reallexikon der ägyptischen Religionsgeschichte*. Berlin, Walter De Gruyter, 1952.

BRUYERE, Bernard, *La tombe n° 1 de Sen-nedjem à Deir el Médineh*. Le Caire, Institut français d'Archéologie orientale, 1959.

BRUYERE, Bernard, *Rapport sur les fouilles de Deir el Médineh (1930)*. Le Caire, Institut français d'Archéologie orientale, 1933 (Tombe n° 359 d'Anherkhaou, pp. 33-70, pll. III-XXIII.)

BUCHER, Paul, *Les textes des tombes de Thoutmosis III et d'Aménophis II*. Le Caire, Institut français d'Archéologie orientale (= Mémoires t. 60), 1932.

CAMPBELL, Colin, *Two Theban Princes, Khaem-Uast and Amen-khepeshf, sons of Ramses III, Menna, a Land-Steward, and their Tombs*. Edinburgh, Oliver and Boyd, 1910.

CARTER, Howard, *The Tomb of Tut-ankh-Amen*, vol. I-III. London, Cassell, 1923-1933.

CERNY, Jaroslav, *Ancient Egyptian Religion*. London, Hutchinson House, 1952.

CERNY, Jaroslav, *A Community of Workmen at Thebes in the Ramesside Period*. Cairo, Institut français d'Archéologie orientale (= Bibliothèque d'Etude 50), 1973.

DAUMAS, François, *La Civilisation de l'Egypte pharaonique*. Paris, Arthaud, 1982.

DAVIES, Nina M., with the editorial assistance of Sir Alan H. GARDINER, *Ancient Egyptian Paintings*, vol. I-II Plates; vol. III Descriptive Text. Chicago, The University of Chicago Press, 1936.

DAVIES, Norman de Garis, *The Tomb of Nakht at Thebes*. New York, Metropolitan Museum of Art, 1917.

DAVIES, Norman de Garis, *The Tomb of Rekh-mi-Re at Thebes*. vol. I-II. New York, Metropolitan Museum of Art, 1943.

DAVIES, Norman de Garis, *The Tomb of the Vizier Ramose*. London, Egypt Exploration Society, 1941.

DAVIES, Norman de Garis, *Two Ramesside Tombs at Thebes*. New York, Metropolitan Museum of Art, 1927.

DESROCHES-NOBLECOURT, Christiane, *Vie et mort d'un pharaon Toutankhamon*. Paris, Hachette, 1963.

DRIOTON, Etienne, et Jacques VANDIER, *Les Peuples de l'Orient méditerranéen, II. L'Egypte*, 4e édition. Paris, Presses Universitaires de France (collection Clio), 1962.

DRIOTON, Etienne, et Pierre du BOURGUET, *Les pharaons à la conquête de l'art*. Bruges, Desclée de Brouwer, 1965.

EGGEBRECHT, Arne, *Das alte Ägypten*. 3000 Jahre Geschichte und Kultur des Pharaonenreiches. München, C. Bertelsmann, 1984.

EGGEBRECHT, Arne, *L'Egypte ancienne au royaume des Pharaons*. Paris, Bordas, 1986.

ERMAN, Adolf, und Hermann RANKE, *Aegypten und aegyptisches Leben im Altertum*. Tübingen, J.C.B. Mohr, 1923.

ERMAN, Adolf, et Hermann RANKE, *La civilisation égyptienne*. Paris, Payot, 1976.

FORNARI, Annamaria, e Mario TOSI, *Nella sede della Verità*. Deir el Medina e l'ipogeo di Thutmosi III. Milano, Franco Maria Ricci, 1987.

GARDINER, Alan H., *The Attitude of the Ancient Egyptians to Death and the Dead*. Cambridge, University Press, 1935.

GOEDICKE, Hans (see *Nofretari*).

GOYON, Jean-Claude, *Rituels funéraires de l'ancienne Egypte*. Paris, Editions du Cerf, 1972.

GRIMAL, Nicolas, *Histoire de l'Egypte ancienne*. Paris, Arthème Fayard, 1988.

HASSANEIN, F(athy), et M(onique) NELSON, *La tombe du Prince Amon-(her)-khepchef*. Le Caire, Centre d'Etudes et de Documentation sur l'ancienne Egypte, 1976.

HORNUNG, Erik, *Das Amduat*. I-III. Wiesbaden, Otto Harrassowitz, 1963-1967.

HORNUNG, Erik, *Das Buch der Anbetung des Re im Westen (Sonnenlitanei)* = Aegyptiaca Helvetica 2-3. Genève, Editions de Belles-Lettres, 1975-1976.

HORNUNG, Erik, *Das Buch von den Pforten des Jenseits* = Aegyptiaca Helvetica 7-8. Genève, Editions de Belles-Lettres, 1979-1980.

HORNUNG, Erik, *Das Grab des Haremhab im Tal der Könige*. Bern, Francke Verlag, 1971.

HORNUNG, Erik, *Das Tal der Könige*. Die Ruhestätte der Pharaonen. Zürich und München, Artemis Verlag, 1982.

HORNUNG, Erik, *Das Totenbuch der Ägypter*. Zürich und München, Artemis Verlag, 1979.

JAMES, T.G.H., *Pharaoh's People*. Scenes from Life in Imperial Egypt. London-Sydney-Toronto, The Bodley Head, 1984.

LECLANT, Jean, Editeur : *Le monde égyptien, les Pharaons* (ouvrage collectif), en 3 volumes : Le temps des Pyramides, l'Empire des conquérants, l'Egypte du crépuscule. Paris, Gallimard (collection L'univers des formes), 1979.

Lexikon der Ägyptologie. I-VI. Wiesbaden, Otto Harrassowitz, 1975-1986.

LHOTE, André, et HASSIA, préface de Jacques VANDIER, *Les chefs-d'oeuvre de la peinture égyptienne.* Paris, Hachette, 1954.

MEKHITARIAN, Arpag, *La peinture égyptienne.* Genève, A. Skira, 1954 et 1978.

MEKHITARIAN, Arpag, *Egyptian Painting.* Geneva, A. Skira, 1954.

MEKHITARIAN, Arpag, *Ägyptische Malerei.* Genf, A. Skira, 1954.

MEKHITARIAN, Arpag, *Religions du monde : l'Egypte.* Paris, Bloud & Gay, 1964.

MICHALOWSKI, Kazimierz, *L'art de l'ancienne Egypte.* Paris, Mazenod, 1968.

MORENZ, Siegfried, *Ägyptische Religion.* Stuttgart, W. Kohlhammer, 1960.

MORENZ, Siegfried, *La religion égyptienne.* Paris, Payot, 1962.

MORENZ, Siegfried, *Gott und Mensch im alten Ägypten*, 2. Auflage. Zürich und München, Artemis Verlag, 1984.

MOSS, Rosalind L.B. (see Bertha PORTER).

NELSON, Monique (see F. HASSANEIN).

Nofretari. Eine Dokumentation der Wandgemälde ihres Grabes (A Documentation of her Tomb and its Decoration). Einleitung (Introduction) Gertrud THAUSING, Kommentar (Commentary) Hans GOEDICKE. Graz, Akademische Druck und Verlaganstalt, 1971.

PECK, William H., *Drawings from ancient Egypt.* London, Thames and Hudson, 1978.

PIANKOFF, Alexandre, *Le Livre du jour et de la nuit.* Le Caire, Institut français d'Archéologie orientale (Bibliothèque d'Etude 13), 1942.

PIANKOFF, Alexandre, *Le Livre des Quererts*, dans "Bulletin de l'Institut français d'Archéologie orientale", tomes 41, 42, 43 et 45. Le Caire, 1942-1945.

PIANKOFF, Alexandre, and N. RAMBOVA, *The Tomb of Ramesses VI*, vol. 1-2 (= Bollingen Series 40, 1). New York, Pantheon Books, 1954.

PORTER, Bertha, Rosalind L.B. MOSS & Ethel W. BURNEY, *Topographical Bibliography of Ancient Egyptian Hieroglyphic Texts, Reliefs and Paintings*, I. The Theban Necropolis. Oxford, Clarendon Press, Part 1, 1960; Part 2, 1964.

POSENER, Georges, Serge SAUNERON et Jean YOYOTTE, *Dictionnaire de la civilisation égyptienne.* Paris, Fernand Hazan, 1959 et 1970.

RANKE, Hermann (see Adolf ERMAN).

SAUNERON, Serge, et Jean YOYOTTE, *La naissance du monde selon l'Egypte ancienne*, dans "Sources Orientales" I. La naissance du monde, p. 17-91. Paris, Seuil, 1959.

SAUNERON, Serge, *Les prêtres de l'ancienne Egypte*, (= Le temps qui court 6). Paris, Seuil, 1957.

SAUNERON, Serge (see also Georges POSENER).

SCHIAPARELLI, E(rnesto), *Relazione sui lavori della Missione archeologica italiana in Egitto* (anni 1903-1920), vol. I, Valle delle Regine; vol. II, La tomba intatta dell' architetto Cha. Torino, R. Museo di Antichità, 1923 e 1927.

Sen-nefer. Die Grabkammer des Bürgermeisters von Theben (Römisch-germanisches Museum Köln). Mainz, Philipp von Zabern, 1986. Also : Ägypten, Götter, Gräber und die Kunst 4000 Jahre Jenseitsglaube, Band II, *Das Grab des Sennefer* (OÖ. Landesmuseum Linz). Mainz, Philipp von Zabern, und Linz, Grosser-Druck, 1989.

SHEDID, Abdel Ghaffar (see Christine BEINLICH-SEEBER).

SPIEGEL, Joachim, *Die Idee vom Totengericht in der ägyptischen Religion* (= Leipziger ägyptische Studien 2). Glückstadt, J.J. Augustin, 1935.

THAUSING, Gertrud (see *Nofretari*).

TOSI, Mario (see Annamaria FORNARI).

VALBELLE, Dominique, *Les ouvriers de la tombe* : Deir el-Médineh à l'époque ramesside. Le Caire, Institut français d'Archéologie orientale (= Bibliothèque d'Etude 96), 1985.

VANDERSLEYEN, Claude, *Das alte Ägypten* (=Propyläen Kunstgeschichte 15). Berlin, Propyläen Verlag, 1975.

VANDIER, Jacques, *La religion égyptienne.* Paris, Presses Universitaires de France (collection Mana), 1944.

VANDIER, Jacques (see also Etienne DRIOTON).

VERGOTE J(ozef), *De Egyptenaren en hun godsdienst*, 2. druk. De Haan, Bussum, 1974.

VERNUS, Pascal, et Jean YOYOTTE, *Les Pharaons.* Paris, MA éditions, 1988.

WILDUNG, Dietrich, *L'âge d'or de l'Egypte, le Moyen Empire.* Fribourg (Suisse), Office du Livre, 1984.

YOYOTTE, Jean, *Le jugement des morts dans l'Egypte ancienne* (= Sources orientales IV. Le jugement des morts, p. 15-80). Paris, Seuil, 1961.

YOYOTTE, Jean (see also Georges POSENER, Serge SAUNERON and Pascal VERNUS).

ZABKAR, Louis V., *A Study of the Ba Concept in Ancient Egyptian Texts* (= Studies in ancient oriental civilization 34). Chicago, University of Chicago Press, 1968.

ACKNOWLEDGEMENTS

In the course of frequent visits to Egypt we nurtured the idea of improving the knowledge of the Theban Necropolis. This slowly maturing project seemed especially worthwhile since the phenomenal boom of tourism made the country more and more accessible to an increasingly interested public.

Egypt is readily associated with the image of the pyramids, but the ancient Egyptian concept of Eternity has also been represented in a fabulous and decidedly human way in the tombs of princes, queens, pharaohs, artisans and nobles, situated on the left bank of the Nile, opposite the temples of Karnak and Luxor.

To avoid having to work in an atmosphere of secretiveness - as, admittedly, we had done before - we eventually, and not in the least thanks to the wonderful assistance of Dr. Hamawy and his wife in Cairo, acquired an authorization from the Egyptian Antiquities Organization to take photographs on the site. Photography in these circumstances not only requires a permit, but, more importantly so, expert precision and a sense of perfection, which fortunately happen to be two of the main concerns of Professor Marc Kunnen, a long time friend and Professor at the Department of Radiology at the University of Ghent. Together with his son, a doctor, we set up a team which worked wonders in the period which had been allocated to us.

Working incessantly from dawn till dusk, we covered some twenty tombs of the Theban Necropolis, bringing back with us a considerable treasure of iconographical material which we then subjected to a rigourous selection. The title of the book, though proposed post factum, was immediately accepted because it perfectly reflected our initial idea, linking the description of the sites to the symbol of eternity omnipresent in Egyptian religion and in the tombs themselves.

A literary structure for the project was gladly provided by Arpag Mekhitarian, Secretary General of the Queen Elisabeth Egyptological Foundation, himself an egyptologist of high repute. Our enthusiasm proved contagious and he tackled the task with his typical, inspiring ardour. This team, composed of individuals from various scientific backgrounds, rallied its forces with that of the publishers, Mappamundi, to ensure that the book would meet the highest standards in the art of book-making. A final word of thanks should be directed towards all those who became involved with the project on a personal, rather than a professional level, and to my wife Odile especially, who had to bear with me even when I was totally absorbed by the preparations for the project.

Nevertheless we are convinced that all efforts combined have yielded a splendid result with this publication and that, through it, our original goal of promoting and safeguarding some of the greatest Egyptian masterpieces for future generations, has been attained.

René WULLEMAN

PHOTO CREDITS

Marc Kunnen :

Pages 17 to 31, 32 (right), 33 to 43, 46, 48 to 51, 54, 56 to 65, 70, 71, 73 to 79, 80 (two at the top), 81, 82, 90 to 101, 105, 106 (bottom), 110, 111 (bottom), 112 to 118, 120, 121, 122 (top), 123 to 127, 144, 146, 148, 149, 154 to 157, 159, 160 (bottom), 162 to 165, 168 to 176.

Arpag Mekhitarian :

Pages 44, 84 to 87, 89, 104, 131 to 143.

René Wulleman :

Front cover and pages 32 (left), 52, 53, 55, 66 to 69, 72, 80 (bottom), 83, 88, 103, 106 (top), 107 to 109, 111 (top), 119, 122 (bottom), 128 to 130, 147, 150 to 153, 158, 160 (top), 161, 166, 167.

TOMBS OF THE KINGS
(East Valley)

1 : 10.000

0   50 100   200 Yards

N

35

1

12

13

14

32

34

21

28

Tombs of the Kings
(West Valley)

Tomb

13

Tombs of the
Queens

Shêkh 'Abd
el Kurna

Dêr el-Medineh

N

S

Tomb of Hui

Kurnet   Murrai

German
House

South Asasif

T. of Ramses III.

Medinet Habu

T. of Thutmosis III.

T. of Merenptah

T. of Tewosret

Ramesse

T. of
Thutmosis IV.

T. of Uazmose

Kom el-Hetan